BILL MCKIBBEN is the author of *The End of Nature* and *The Age of Missing Information*, which is available in Plume. A former staff writer for *The New Yorker*, he is a frequent contributor to such publications as the *New York Times*, *The New York Review of Books*, and *Outside* magazine. He lives with his wife and daughter in upstate New York.

Praise for *The Age of Missing Information*

"McKibben grasps the nature of television,
and does so brilliantly."
—*New York Times Book Review*

"Invigorating, revelatory . . . what television tells—
and doesn't tell—about the world we live in."
—*Time*

"Masterful . . . a unique, bizarre portrait of our life
and times."
—*Los Angeles Times*

"A brilliantly lucid and effective challenge to the myth
of the Information Age, McKibben's book persuades us
that there is another real world out there that also broad-
casts around the clock and that it has the power to
transform us if we can stand still long enough to
listen to its faint and ancient call."
—*Kirkus Reviews*

"Do yourself a favor: Put down the remote and
pick up this book."
—*Houston Chronicle*

"This book is so well thought out and written, it's
bound to make couch potatoes uneasy."
—*Christian Science Monitor*

"By turns humorous, wise, and troubling . . .
a penetrating critique of technological society."
—*Cleveland Plain Dealer*

Praise for *The End of Nature*

"By the 'end of nature' Mr. McKibben means the end of
nature as a force independent of man . . . For a man
preaching apocalypse, he speaks in a measured and
civilized voice that deserves a hearing."
—*New York Times Book Review*

"Bill McKibben's subject is the end of nature itself, which
he claims humans have already brought about. The
subject is important, the notion is arresting, and
Mr. McKibben argues convincingly."
—*Wall Street Journal*

"A thoughtful book by a fine writer."
—*San Francisco Examiner*

"A dark and unsettling account of the abuse we've
done to our environment and of the unprecedented
effects—both physical and philosophical—it is going
to have on our future."
—*Vanity Fair*

"You must read *The End of Nature*. You mustn't be
happy about it, but please read it. It's a great and
terrible work, like few that have been written."
—Rick Bass, author of *Oil Notes*

"[McKibben] may well already have taken his place
next to Rachel Carson and *Silent Spring*."
—*Baltimore Evening Sun*

"Too gripping to lay down."
—*Dallas Morning News*

ALSO BY BILL McKIBBEN

The Age of Missing Information

The End of Nature

Hope, Human and Wild

maybe
one

A Case for Smaller Families

BILL McKIBBEN

A PLUME BOOK

PLUME
Published by the Penguin Group
Penguin Putnam Inc., 375 Hudson Street, New York, New York 10014, U.S.A.
Penguin Books Ltd, 27 Wrights Lane, London W8 5TZ, England
Penguin Books Australia Ltd, Ringwood, Victoria, Australia
Penguin Books Canada Ltd, 10 Alcorn Avenue, Toronto, Ontario,
  Canada M4V 3B2
Penguin Books (N.Z.) Ltd, 182–190 Wairau Road, Auckland 10, New Zealand

Penguin Books Ltd, Registered Offices: Harmondsworth, Middlesex, England

10 9 8 7 6 5 4 3

Ⓟ REGISTERED TRADEMARK—MARCA REGISTRADA

The Library of Congress has catalogued the hardcover edition as follows:
McKibben, Bill.
  Maybe one : a case for smaller families / Bill McKibben.
    p.   cm.
ISBN 0-684-85281-0
      0-452-28092-3(pbk.)
  1. Population—Environmental aspects. 2. Overpopulation. 3. Nature—Effect of
human beings on. 4. Environmental degradation—Social aspects. 5. Family size.
  1. Title. II. Title: Maybe 1.
HB849.415.M39   1998
304.2—DC21   98-5417
                                                                   CIP

Designed by Ruth Lee

BOOKS ARE AVAILABLE AT QUANTITY DISCOUNTS WHEN USED TO PROMOTE PRODUCTS OR SER-
VICES. FOR INFORMATION PLEASE WRITE TO PREMIUM MARKETING DIVISION, PENGUIN PUTNAM
INC., 375 HUDSON STREET, NEW YORK, NEW YORK 10014.

For my godchildren,
Gordie, Annie, and Micah,
and for their brothers and sisters,
Alice, Johnny, Nora, Christopher, and Chloe;
and for the many, many children of the
Johnsburg and Mill Creek United Methodist
Church Sunday School

Contents

Contents

Introduction

Population is a subject I've been trying to avoid for years, and not just because I know it will cause turmoil and angry controversy. It scared me more because it forced me and my wife to confront head-on the issue of how many children we were going to have, a decision that probably affects each of our lives more than any we will ever make. It's as intimate a topic as there is, one of the last subjects we avoid in this taboo-free society. At some level, it's not any of my business how many kids anyone else has.

And yet my work on environmental issues kept bringing questions of population front and center. For reasons I will explain at some length, the next fifty years will be crucial to our planet's future—they are the years that could so devastate the earth's biology that it will never again be able to support life as abundantly as it does at present. How many people we have on this planet during that half-century—especially in its richest sections—will go a long way toward determining how deep that damage is.

Americans currently bear children at a rate of just under two per woman, which sounds like we should simply be replacing ourselves. But, happily, most of us do not die soon after becoming parents; we live on to see our kids reproduce, and perhaps their kids. Combined with unprecedentedly high levels of immigration, the Census Bureau says this rate of natural increase will bring our population of 270 million to as many as 400 million in those crucial fifty years, that by the year 2050 there will be almost 50 percent more of us than there are right now. These numbers are guesses, forecasts; the Census Bureau revises them regularly as fertility and immigration change. But by even the most conservative estimates, from columnists like Ben Wattenberg, our nation's population will grow at least 30 percent in the next half-century. It is true, as I will show, that rates of global population growth have begun to slow, and that the peak of our numbers may be within (distant) sight. It is, unfortunately, also true that that peak is too far off to stave off our environmental troubles, and that the United States in particular continues to grow far faster than other industrialized nations.

But if we averaged 1.5 children per woman—if, that is, many more people decided to stop at one child, nudging the birthrate down toward the current European level—and if we simultaneously reduced immigration somewhat, then in the year 2050 our population would be about 230 million, or what it was when Ronald Reagan was elected. I'm not saying, then, that everyone should stop at one child; just that if many more of us did so, it would help. That gap of as many as 170 million Americans could be crucial, I think, in reducing our environmental damage. By itself it would not solve the problem, for our fierce appetites and our old-fashioned fossil-fuel technologies also account for much of our dilemma. But it would make a difference.

To be honest, though, that's not the real reason I did the research for this book. I did it because of Sophie, my four-year-old daughter. I wanted to make sure that growing up without brothers and sisters would not damage her spirit or her mind. That's why the first chapters of this book have nothing to do with the environment and everything to do with kids.

And it's why the last chapter—after all the discussion of demographics and global warming and Social Security and immigration—focuses on parents, on me and my wife and anyone else grappling with what it might mean to raise much smaller families than tradition dictates, or to raise no families at all.

Those considerations—of children and of parents, of our offspring and of our souls—bracket the more traditional argument this book contains. They will serve, I hope, to make what has usually been an abstract question very personal and immediate. I do not doubt that that will make this book even more disturbing to readers who disagree with me. But that is as it should be, for my desire is to open a debate, to get a conversation going.

This particular debate, however, can quickly deteriorate into a shrill and bitter tussle. So I want to begin by listing a few things I am *not* saying in this book, secure in the knowledge that there are plenty more issues that will—and should—be contested.

I'm not saying that my friends, or anyone else, are wrong to have several children, or that they should feel guilty or defensive. As I've already said, I don't think it's necessary for every family to have but a single child. There are plenty of good reasons to have children, chief among them that kids are magnificent. This volume is dedicated to my godchildren and their brothers and sisters, as well as to the dozens of first, second, third, and fourth children I've had the pleasure of teaching in my Sunday School class over the years. There are also a dozen categories of grief and joy—divorce, remarriage, adoption, and so forth—that I've not covered in these very basic calculations. All I'm saying is that we live at a watershed moment in our ecological history when we need at least to *consider* this question, a question that we almost never talk about. We have dozens of books about how to raise children, where to send them to college, even what to name them; this is no less practical a topic.

And I'm not saying that our governments should coerce us into reducing the size of our families. That's repugnant and it's unnecessary; we've barely begun to think about population in this country, and I think it's likely that once the discussion begins we can develop some new social norms on our own, through gradual shifts in what's counted as desirable.

I'm not saying that population is a problem for some other kind of people—Tanzanians or poor people or teenage welfare mothers. Because we live so large, North Americans (and Europeans and Asians of the quickly growing industrial powers) will largely determine what shape the world is in fifty years hence. Tanzanians can make their own lives more difficult through rapid population growth, but they can do very little to damage the basic fabric of the planet.

And by the same token, I don't consider population to be *the* problem, though that is what zealots have sometimes claimed. In the past I've written about overconsumption and about efficiency, topics that will recur in this book. It is essential that we consume less, and consume more intelligently—that we live in smaller homes, and heat them with sun and wind. But, as we shall see, if the population keeps increasing those difficult changes will be robbed of much of their meaning.

I'm not saying this is a problem for women, though that's where the burden of decision-making about family size has usually fallen. It's a question for both halves of any couple, and sometimes for grandparents and friends—and in our case the conversation ended with me in a vasectomy clinic.

And of course I'm not trying to pretend that single-child families are a solution that raises no problems. Conservative critics like the American Enterprise Institute's Nicholas Eberstadt have warned, correctly, that the world will *feel* very different to only kids as they age. A nation with a stable population will clearly have an economy very different from a rapidly growing one. And our nation will age more rapidly than it otherwise would, making it even harder to deal with things like shortfalls in Social Security. Some of this book is devoted to dealing with those problems, and some of it with arguing that they are small compared with the environmental troubles we face. But they are real, and won't be wished away.

I'm not saying—crucially—that single-child families are a permanent solution. Clearly, they're not; eventually they would yield populations smaller than almost anyone would want. If I could write this book on paper that erased itself in fifty years, I would; by the middle of the next century our populations, our technologies, our desires, our predicaments may be fundamentally different. Perhaps we will want to unleash another baby boom; perhaps not. There is no way to predict. But should you happen across a yellowing copy of this book in that future time, regard it as merely a historical curiosity.

Finally, I'm not even saying that I'm right. For a long time

Sue and I considered having no children. As I wrote a decade ago in *The End of Nature*, when we were first struggling with the issue, "we try very hard not to think about how much we'd like a baby." Thank God we kept thinking, kept wanting, for Sophie is the great joy of our lives. This time, with the help of the surgeon, we've made up our minds for good. But that does not mean our doubts vanish.

In any event, my hope is not to settle this question for anyone else; it truly isn't my business what you choose to do. All I want is to open a debate, to remove "population" from the category of abstraction and make it the very real consideration of how many children you or I may decide to bear. No single decision any of us will make will mean as much to our own lives or to the life of the planet.

PART ONE

FAMILY

chapter one

 I T WAS ONE OF THOSE NIGHTS THAT DIDN'T GO SO WELL. MAYBE BEDTIME CAME A LITTLE LATE, MAYBE SHE WAS HUNGRY. WHATever the reason, our wonderful and capable and smart and kind daughter sat in her room sobbing, unable to cope with putting on her pajamas. We finally got her tucked in, finally got the stories told, the songs sung, finally repaired to the couch for the postmortem. There is nothing so strong in my life as the desire that my daughter be happy, healthy, whole; no worry as profound as that I may somehow screw her up.

• • •

Compared with the other prejudices that haunt our age, the bias against only children seems hardly worth mentioning. No one is denied a job for being an only child; no one moves out if one moves in down the block.

And yet the lingering suspicion that only children are likely to be "different"—selfish, spoiled, maladjusted loners—

carries real consequences. When surveyed, parents say the single biggest reason for having a second child is to provide their firstborn with a sibling.[1] It's a hardy piece of folk wisdom; even parents like my wife and me who decide to stick with one worry that growing up alone will warp our children. It makes a certain amount of intuitive sense, after all—with so many more hours spent in the company of adults or by themselves, you'd think that only children might be bookish or asocial or a little odd. Stereotypes can grow from truths.

So I needed to find out for sure. If it's true, if only children really *are* damaged by the experience of growing up without brothers or sisters, then even compelling environmental arguments about the size of our population will go unheeded. What parent would volunteer to make their child miserable in order to reduce infinitesimally the amount of carbon dioxide in the atmosphere? If it's true, then maybe Sue and I need to think more about another child. If it's true, then this book would be nonsense: given a choice between a nation composed of 230 million selfish brats and 400 million well-adjusted people, I know which I'd choose.

And anyway, it makes for a pretty good detective story.

•   •   •

It's as rare to see the birth of a prejudice as it is to watch the birth of a star—most come from so deep in the past that it's hard to imagine there was a time when they didn't exist. But the idea that only children are damaged seems to be of modern provenance. Until recent times only children were a rarity. Perhaps a small family represented a problem for the parents, those semi-barren unfortunates who would have to depend on a single young man or woman to support them as they aged. But very few people paid much attention to child psychology, to child development. It wasn't until the end of the last century that an American researcher, a man named G. Stanley Hall, declared that "being an only child is a disease in itself."[2]

Granville Stanley Hall, born in 1844 in a Massachusetts farming town, is one of those figures who has sunk beneath the waves of history. And yet in his day he was a mighty eminence—the creator at Johns Hopkins of the first American research laboratory in psychology, the leading educational reformer of his time, the founder of one of the nation's first research universities. He knew everyone, and everyone knew him. Freud, for instance, first came to America at Hall's invitation. (Jung came along with him and on the trip claimed to have witnessed Freud wetting his pants; his attempt to analyze the event for the master led, Jung said, to the break between them.)[3] Soon after Freud and Jung arrived at Hall's house, William James, an old friend of Hall's, knocked on the door with *his* suitcase.[4]

Hall cared most about understanding the growth of children, and he launched and nurtured a vast national enterprise known as the "child-study movement." In 1882 he urged the by-now-obvious idea that the stages of a child's development "must be the basis of methods of teaching, topics chosen, and their order." The next year he published a pioneering study, "The Content of Children's Minds," that tried to figure out what kids might be "assumed to know and have seen by their teachers when they enter school."[5] He made serious study of children at play,[6] introduced eye and hearing tests as a standard part of the school program,[7] and spread the gospel that "constant muscular activity was natural for the child, and, therefore, the immense effort of the drillmaster teachers to make children sit still was harmful and useless." He even, as part of his early studies of cliques and groups among children, "defended the street gangs of the slums as wholesome if they could be diverted from their criminal activities."[8]

He was, in other words, well ahead of his time. And he was greeted with great acclaim—there were even Hall Clubs to spread his work. He was a sort of Victorian Dr. Spock. But these were also the earliest days of the social sciences, before fields like psychology had settled down to what we consider the routines of research. People were still feeling their way. William James, for instance, was obsessed with what we'd now call the occult, the New Age. When he arrived at Hall's house to greet Freud, he was carrying reprints of his recent article about a series of séances conducted by the professional medium Mrs. Leonore Piper.[9] Hall, to his credit, was skeptical of all that. He tried hard to do real research. The trouble was, no one really knew how to do research yet.

After months of searching, in a cavernous basement of the State University of New York library in Albany, I finally came across the bound volumes of the first journal Hall published, the *Pedagogical Seminary*. The dry, cracked leather of the bindings hadn't been opened in many years, but they were utterly fascinating to read—a portrait of a profession in its earliest years, before graduate students and professors had learned what to study and what to leave alone. Whatever an academic published in the *Pedagogical Seminary* was likely to be the first work ever written on the topic. Footnotes are few and far between, grand summations common. Most of the authors appear to be Stanley Hall protégés, many from his newly founded Clark University. G. E. Partridge, for instance, writes a monograph on "second breath or second wind," based on some survey responses "turned over to me by Dr. Hall." ("Case 4. Female. 16. 'I have been to receptions when I have danced nearly every set until about 11 o'clock. When I stopped I would feel as though I couldn't dance another set, but when asked to dance the next, I accepted, and danced until my tired feeling left me.'") There are papers such as "Memory in School Children" ("It seems that memory power for boys culminates about the beginning of the high school period") and "The Child and the Weather" ("abnormal movement of wind, as shown by maximum velocity, seems to increase misdemeanors twenty percent") and on a hundred other topics of interest to educators.

But the blockbuster piece of research, the gold mine that yielded numerous papers, including the findings on only children, was entitled "A Study of Peculiar and Exceptional Children." It began innocently enough. In 1895, Hall mailed a questionnaire to college instructors in several states, asking them to submit reports on unusual children. These did not have to be current pupils; teachers were also invited to "think back over your own childhood," to "consider if you have any friends" who were exceptional, to ask their better students to "describe one or more such cases in a composition," and even to report "any exceptional children you ever read of, whether fact or fiction." He then assigned a graduate student, E. W. Bohannon, to digest the results, which soon numbered 1,045 cases—850 from Miss Lillie A. Williams of the New Jersey State Normal School, others from Farmington, Maine; Evanston, Indiana; and "35 or 40 from personal sources of friends. Every report bears evidence of sincerity, and practically all of thoughtful, careful preparation."

This data base, enormous for the time, was divided into those children who were peculiar and exceptional for *physical* reasons ("exceptional beauty or ugliness, . . . conspicuous scars or traumatic lesions . . . clumsiness and deftness, etc.") and for *psychical* reasons ("daintiness or gluttony, . . . frankness or secretiveness . . . a buffoon; a restless, fickle, scatterbrained or tenacious child; a dignified or self-poised child," and so on). Each child's nationality, age, sex, complexion, and temperament were also listed, as well as the reporter's assessment of "whether the trait is hereditary, how far back it can be traced, and how marked it was in the ancestry."

Hall's protégé Bohannon then digested many of the reports, so his readers could see for themselves the value of the data. Under the category HEAVY, for example, we find an account of an eight-year-old who weighed a hundred pounds ("Girls often call her 'Mutton Chops' on account of her stoutness"); under SMALL a ten-year-old boy who weighed 43 pounds ("One day when a strong wind was blowing he did not reach school until late, because he had to wait until some one found and carried him in"); under STRONG an eighteen-year-old fair-skinned girl who "lifted a corner of the piano up while her mother put the leg in," and under DEFT a "generous and good-natured" ten-and-a-half-year-old who "made 175 peach baskets in nine hours." For sixty pages he describes the CLUMSY ("Mother had some small ducks and chickens in the yard, and every time K. went out she was sure to kill one by stepping on it"), the UGLY ("F. 9 yrs. old. Light. Nervous. Ugliest person ever seen. Looks like a monkey"), the DEFORMED ("right ear is simply a roll of cartilage about one inch long and no opening"). Some children have BIRTHMARKS ("A very decided spot on her left hand. She found that by rubbing it, it might be made to disappear for an instant, and will sit rubbing it by the hour"), while others have SENSE KEENNESS ("M. 4 yrs. old. Could smell onions in the house where they had been cooked day before") or SPEECH DEFECTS ("M. 10 yrs. old. American. Florid. Inclined to leave out unimportant words in speaking. . . . Father a butcher and boy probably eats much meat") or are NERVOUS ("harsh words affect her deeply").

On the list goes, through the CLEAN, the DAINTY ("won't eat any kind of pie but pumpkin"), the OBEDIENT, the DISOBEDIENT, the DIRTY ("M. 5 yrs. old. Eats dirty grass, pretending to be a horse"), the DISORDERLY, the BUOYANT, the TEASING ("M. 4 yrs. old. Took the lemon squeezer out and put a kitten in it. When kitten mewed, he laughed") and the BUFFOONS ("F. 14 yrs. old. Dark. Rolled her eyeballs so as to show only the whites"). Some of the children sound about as unexceptional as it is possible to sound: under SELFISH there's a thirteen-year-old with light skin who, "several times when she had candy given her, . . . ran upstairs and hid it where none but herself could find it," and under SYMPATHY we read of several children who cannot stand to see animals suffer, as well as one who is "always picking up bugs and such things." Some are ILL-TEMPERED ("when sick would dash away medicine in a fury"); some are LOQUACIOUS; some are TIMID ("M. 6 yrs. old. American. Very bright and well-formed. Afraid of toads"); some are COURAGEOUS ("F. 8 yrs. old. Norwegian. Will go to bed in any room, no matter how dark. Her mother never allowed her to be told any ghost stories or to hear of hell, hence she knows no fear"). He concludes with the GLUTTONOUS ("F. 1½ yrs. old. Light. Saw her eat two dishes of apple sauce, oysters, crackers, milk, and cry for cheese and bananas").

All of these children are duly catalogued, arranged into neat statistical tables that demonstrate beyond all possible nineteenth-century doubt a number of important conclusions. For instance, immigrant children are overrepresented among the peculiar—"over half the non-American element is found in the group having disadvantageous traits," a danger that increases if two parents who have immigrated from *different* countries make the mistake of marrying.

For our purposes, however, the most important finding is

that 46 of the 1,045 total cases are only children, "a number entirely out of proportion to that found among children generally. The only child in a family is therefore very likely to be peculiar and exceptional."[10]

So peculiar, in fact, as to warrant further study. A year later, Bohannon returns to the pages of the *Pedagogical Seminary* with a more detailed breakdown of the data in his article "The Only Child in a Family." He sends out across the nation for more case studies; again Miss Lillie Williams of New Jersey provides more than half the cases. The only children are grouped by their HEALTH ("takes cold easily and cannot stand much hardship"; "subject to severe headaches, and in the winter time to bronchitis and croup"), their RELATION TO SCHOOL ("He did excellent school work, but instead of playing he would sit in the Navy Yard and examine machinery"), their PLAY AND SOCIAL LIFE ("F., 11. American-Jew. Nervous. At home she places books on chairs as her pupils and, with another book in her hand, she addresses the chairs as her pupils"), and of course their MENTAL AND MORAL PECULIARITIES ("When she plays with other children she gets along with them reasonably well, but she does not care to run or take part in active sports"). From these, many conclusions are drawn: not only do only children frequently contract a disease called "St. Vitus Dance" and display an uncommon number of harelips, flat feet, and pigeon toes, they also tend to get along badly with others, not do well in school, and create imaginary companions. Mr. Bohannon ends with the following helpful epigraph, from an article in the November 7, 1896, issue of the *Spectator*.

> It will be noticed that all creatures which have large families, whether beasts or birds, have less trouble in rearing them

than those which have only one or two young. Little pigs
are weeks ahead of young calves, and the young partridge,
with its dozen brothers and sisters, is far more teachable
than the young eagle.[11]

It's easy to discover the ideology, to give it a dignified
name, behind these studies. G. Stanley Hall, as he makes clear
in an autobiographical essay he wrote for the American Antiquarian Society in 1892, spent the best summers of his boy-
hood "with a large family on a large farm in Ashfield,"
Massachusetts. Later in life, he spent his vacations revisiting
those haunts, interviewing the oldest inhabitants, and "col-
lecting old farm tools, household utensils, furniture, articles of
dress, and hundreds of miscellaneous old objects." He is
among the original nostalgists, and his firm conviction is that
this even-then vanishing world of crosscut saws, drawknives,
flails, fish poles, cheese hoops, "weather vanes in the form of
fish," looms, harnesses, "snow-balling," "pathetic negro
melodies," herbal remedies, hourglasses, and turtle eggs was
"the best educational environment for boys at a certain stage
of their development ever realized in history" as well as "the
ideal basis of a state of citizen voters as contemplated by the
framers of our institutions."[12] Every study and survey he did
reflected this belief. When he tried to gauge "The Content of
Children's Minds," for instance, "the general knowledge Hall
asked of the children was of the kind far more accessible to
children raised in the country rather than the city, and he thus
turned up very high rates of ignorance.... Parents should
take their children for visits to the countryside, Hall said, to
improve their intelligence."[13] As with rural life, so with family
life. He'd spent his summers in a "large family" and with a
gang of other local boys, so that had to be the best way, and a

study that seemed to prove it had to be a good study, even if it was the ludicrous mess that he and Bohannon published, with its birthmarks and lesions lumped in with nervousness and daintiness, with its lessons from partridge broods and with its absolutely firm conclusions: "These only children are unmistakably below the average in health and vitality."[14]

I've not discussed this study at such length because it's so intellectually powerful—it obviously violates every rule that any modern social scientist would observe. It is ANECDOTAL, LAME-BRAINED, and MEANINGLESS. But for more than thirty years it was the *only* piece of research on the question of only children, and hence dominated the field by default. When Norman Fenton of the California Bureau of Juvenile Research wrote a paper in 1928 for the *Journal of Genetic Psychology*, the sole scholarly study he could find was Hall and Bohannon's. And he could trace its influence in every popular discussion of the issue in the intervening decades. Books written for parents and teachers cited the study and went on to say things such as: "The only child is greatly handicapped. He cannot be expected to go through life with the same capacity for adjustment that a child reared in the family with other children can be." Or, "If through some misfortune there can be no other child in the family, another should be adopted in order that the child may have a companion." The year before Fenton published his article, the mass-circulation magazine *Liberty* ran an attack on only children illustrated with a drawing of a boy seated on a throne with a scepter in his hand and the enslaved family doing homage. "It would be best for the individual and the race if there were no only children," concluded one expert.[15]

Those thirty years were crucial; the idea of psychology seeped into the public mind for the first time, often as a series of persistent caricatures. And so the notion that only children were psychologically abnormal sank in deeply: "The belief that being an only child is a significant handicap appears to be so generally accepted that academic psychologists suggest it is a 'cultural truism'—an unchallengeable given," reports researcher Judith Blake.[16] The attitudes persist through the present day: As *U.S. News & World Report* wrote in 1994, "child-rearing experts . . . have never been hesitant to warn parents about the perils of siring a single child." (And who, in fact, did the magazine quote? G. Stanley Hall, almost exactly a century after his original study.)[17] Susan Newman, in her book *Parenting an Only Child*, reports that virtually all the parents of only children that she talked to reported being pressured to have a second; in fact, she listed the nine most common pitches that friends and grandparents employed, ranging from "He needs a brother or sister" and "Give him a playmate" to "What kind of parents are you to deprive your child of a sibling?" and "You're being selfish."[18] A past president of the Planned Parenthood Federation of America said she experienced more pressure to have a second child than to have her first.[19]

When people found out I was writing about population, they often said they thought that "priests" were the problem, that religious injunctions against birth control prevented many from even considering small families. As I will explain in some detail later, this is almost certainly not the case; and in any event, the religious arguments are often more subtle and interesting than the standard caricatures. It's not the priests, I think—it's the psychologists. A century of repeated warnings have turned those early studies into conventional wisdom. By now, everyone more or less *knows* that only children are likely to be lonely oddballs. And knowing that, of course, they can find lonely oddballs to confirm their idea. So the question is, can so much conventional wisdom be wrong?

•   •   •

And the answer is yes. Beginning with Norman Fenton's paper in the late 1920s, almost from the moment that psychologists began to do reputable studies of only children, the data began to undermine old Dr. Hall and his baroque collection of the Peculiar and the Exceptional.

The twentieth century saw many explosions, of course, but few more dramatic than the explosion in People Studying Things. As a result, for example, we can state with considerable confidence that babies who will eventually turn out to be only children move, cry, burp, and sneeze more at three months of age than children who will later acquire siblings, although they are somewhat less likely to be fed by spoon. ("These differences were significant for spoon feeding [Z = 2.20, p = .03].")[20]

Let's look at the most basic measures first, the statistics that for better or for worse mark virtually every student who's set foot in a schoolhouse. A twenty-year tracking study of 3,000 high school students demonstrated that only children have higher IQs than their peers with one sibling[21]—in fact, "there are marked negative effects on IQ of increasing sib size."[22] If you test the vocabularies of only children, they'll score nine points higher than children from families with seven or more children; "only children remained significantly superior in average vocabulary performance to children in all other family sizes," even those with just two kids.[23]

As with intelligence, so with achievement. Those from small families go about a year further in school, on average, than those from large families, and only children finish 13.5 years of education, compared with about 13.2 years for the kids with one brother or sister.[24] Not only that, while they're in class they're more confident: when singleton high school sophomores were asked "How do you rate yourself in school ability?" their "index of confidence" was markedly higher than those of any other children. Once they've graduated, they do just as well in the real world—their "occupational prestige" and those of their spouses revealed no significant difference. Not only that, they make as much money.[25] If you want anecdotal evidence, which is to say if you want to play G. Stanley Hall, here's some of the highest grade: disproportionate numbers of only borns have had their faces on the cover of *Time*.[26]

It's easy to guess some of the reasons only children do well in school. With lots of kids, reports Judith Blake, the overall intellectual level of the home becomes more "childlike. . . . Children may saturate the environment in large families so that it may be rare for adult conversations, vocabulary, and interest to hold sway."[27] And since effective studying "typically requires concentrated periods of solitude, the development of a tolerance for being alone at an early age may be helpful to the academic development" of only children.[28]

But the biggest reason—and the most difficult one to discuss, for it makes parents nervous—is that as more children enter the family, there's a dilution in resources. Money, yes, but more important, the parents' time and emotional and physical energy.[29] Everyone tries to give their second, third, or fourth child just as much attention as their first, but there are only so many hours in the day, only so much stress a father can tolerate, only so many Frisbees a mother can throw. I grew up down the block from a family of six—the older boys were among my best friends, and the family was as solid and successful as any I've known, an argument for having lots of kids. But I remember that when the youngest asked to see pictures of himself as a baby, there weren't any around. (Happily, he looked a lot like his older brothers, so their early snapshots could be pressed into service.)

Clipboard-toting researchers have followed mothers around as assiduously as biologists tracking grizzlies, and their exhaustive studies confirm what any new mother of a second child could tell you for free. "The birth of the second child was associated with a decrease in the frequency of the mother's initiation of periods of joint play, attention, and conversational episodes, and with an increase in the frequency of prohibitive commands."[30] That is to say, the VCR becomes increasingly useful when you're trying to nurse a new baby, and you're more likely to just say "No!" when you've slept two hours the night before. Firstborns react by becoming more demanding, and with "increases in sleeping, toilet, and feeding problems."[31] That is, all of a sudden your carefully trained three-year-old suddenly wants to wear a diaper again. On the other hand, "increases in autonomous behavior were also found."[32] Which is to say, with less of you to go around, they figure out how to amuse themselves.

Some of the findings are more specific. Children from small families are read to more than those from large families, "in spite of the fact that children from large families presumably had siblings who could have performed this service."[33] (Having spent approximately ten seconds of my childhood reading to my younger brother, this does not entirely surprise me.) Poring over the records from a health clinic, one researcher discovered that while only borns were just as likely to be referred there in the first place, they were twice as likely to be brought back for follow-up visits.[34]

And then there is my favorite study, titled "Some American Families at Dinner." Two Rutgers professors asked families to run a video camera at mealtime, explaining that "we were interested in recording the kinds of things they did at mealtime and . . . to try as much as possible to go about their 'normal' business, as if the camera were not present." (Predictably, this request met with varied success. "For example, one father became quite angry when his son took a long time eating and was fooling around with his food. The father raised his voice and said, 'Stop messing with your food!' and then after a pause during which it appeared he recalled the camera, he began speaking again—'And the reasons why you should not . . .'" Younger children were less inhibited by the camera. "For example, one 3-year-old target child announced in the middle of the meal, 'Daddy, I have to go make.' The mother said, 'I knew this would happen,' while the father was obliged to take his son to the bathroom.") Once they'd gotten the tapes, the researchers diligently coded "the amount of time each family member spoke to and received vocal input from every other family member." At first, "the coders found it difficult to watch the families larger than size 4 because of the great amount of speaker overlap and general chaos," which probably should have told them something right there. Also, "a good deal of time was spent not talking but eating."

The researchers persevered, however, and they did make some interesting discoveries. First of all, the length of "dinnertime itself does not increase as a function of family size," even though "one might have suspected that more people would talk more and take more time to eat." (One might have expected it, unless one considered the Cub Scout Meeting Effect and the Soccer Playoffs Syndrome.) Neither did the "duration or amount of conversation at dinnertime increase with family size." Everyone talks less and gets talked to less; this "decrease in the quantity of dyad conversation may be related to verbal stimulation level in the parent-child subsystem and may in part be responsible for the finding of an IQ decrease with increasing family size."[35] Keep all that in mind as you dine tonight.

What happens in a family as you have additional children? Psychologists say that the oldest is "dethroned," knocked off the pedestal where she's been—well, where she's been her entire life. This is not such a terrible event; many of us have survived it, and in the process learned certain lessons. But it *is* a boot camp, no question, and the child's first reaction is to become more, not less, dependent—in "a free play laboratory setting" they cry more and cling to their moms.[36] It's hard for kids, and it's hard for parents, even those thrilled about a new baby. "The anguish with which parents face this question of giving up the love affair with their first child in order to share it with a second is surprisingly painful," writes T. Berry Brazelton.[37]

If it is so painful, asks Susan Newman, author of *Parenting an Only Child*, then why do it? There are dozens of answers, many of them quite good. Some concern the parents—their happy memories of brothers and sisters, their intuitive sense that their family is not yet complete, or that all their eggs are in one basket, that an only child is simply "too precious." We'll consider these eventually, in the last chapter of this book. But there are other reasons, too, these having to do with kids. Parents often have second children to help make sure that their first will turn out *normal*. Most parents, after all, aren't *really* concerned about IQ or vocabulary scores or reading levels. They want to know: Will my child be happy? Will my child be weird?

All things being equal, I'd like my daughter to go to Harvard. But what do I really care about? That she's able to mix with the other kids when she goes to *camp*.

Cheaper by the Dozen is one of those books so delightful that everyone who's read it can remember scenes: Frank Gilbreth, the efficiency expert, teaching his brood of twelve children how to bathe in under a minute, or pretending he was the superintendent of an orphanage, or blowing his whistle for family assembly. "We're going to have a wonderful life," he told his bride Lillie on their wedding day. "A wonderful life and a wonderful family. A great big family."

"We'll have children all over the house," Mother smiled. "From the basement to the attic."

"From the floorboards to the chandelier."

"When we go for our Sunday walk we'll look like Mr. and Mrs. Pied Piper."

"How many would you say we should have, just an estimate?" Mother asked.

"Just as an estimate, many."

"Lots and lots."

"We'll sell out for an even dozen," Dad said. "No less. What do you say to that."

"I say," said Mother, "a dozen would be just right. No less."[38]

You could not read *Cheaper by the Dozen* and not long for an enormous family of your own. And you couldn't watch *The Brady Bunch* without thinking it looked like an awful lot of fun. Not to mention *The Partridge Family, Eight Is Enough, The Waltons,* and a dozen other tributes to the large family. It's fine to have single parents on TV, but single children are scarce— call it the *My Three Sons* rule. Those images define normalcy for us, so it's no wonder that we worry kids who grow up without siblings might be different, might be strange. Compared to the Brady Bunch, a desk full of psychological studies are so much gossamer and fluff.

And there are plenty of concrete reasons to worry, too. After all, only children miss some experiences. They never have the chance to care for a new infant, or to be taken care of by an older brother or sister. "Interactions between a first-born child and a new sibling as young as eight months old are found to be complex, varied, and different from the interactions that children have with their parents," said researchers from the Rutgers Institute for the Study of Child Development. Hell, I've seen amazing interactions between children and their siblings when those siblings are *still in Mommy's tummy*. Even from the viewpoint of an environmentalist, it's good if people figure out as soon as possible that they're not the only ones in the world.

Only children probably acquire adult ways of behaving more quickly than kids with siblings, simply because they hang around more with their parents. This is a mixed blessing. Breathes there a parent who hasn't said, "Grow up"? Breathes there a parent who hasn't thought sadly that their child was growing up too fast? The only child may have playmates, but they aren't exactly like brothers or sisters—she has "no prior emotional claim for attention or support" on them.[39] Researchers find only kids have "a more internal locus of control"; with the "constant reinforcement" of attentive parents, they develop "a strong tendency to take responsibility for outcomes."[40] On the other hand, their relationship with their parents may be more tense—Mom and Dad are by definition first-time parents, both anxious and ignorant about child rearing. And if Mom and Dad have decided that they're stopping at one child, they may be all the more likely to smother their kid. "You're so connected to your single being that you feel every hurt, every slight," writes Susan Newman. "Neighborhood teenagers knocked over her snowman and broke her sled; she wasn't invited to a classmate's birthday party. . . . If you have a singleton, you can immerse yourself totally in her distress."[41] And you can immerse yourself totally in her success as well, "hothousing" your child, pushing her with premature challenges. In the words of a psychologist who is an only child and the mother of an only child, "if you put all your eggs in one basket, you want the basket to be special."[42]

The point is, both psychological theory and common sense would lead you to believe that only kids should be different, at least a little. Not necessarily worse off, not necessarily better— the differences cut both ways. (He has no sister to play with; he has no sister to fight with. She doesn't learn to share Dad; she doesn't need to share Dad.) But *different.* So the question is, do these differences lead to trouble? If you look carefully at only children, do you find them to have been damaged by the experience? Are they *very* different, and in ways that make them unhappy? *Are they weird? Are they spoiled?*

•   •   •

Toni Falbo and I met for a drink in the lobby of the Washington hotel where the Population Association of America was holding its annual meeting. Around us swirled academics, on their way to symposia about everything from welfare reform to suburban sprawl. Falbo was giving her own lecture the next day, but at the moment she was talking about herself. "My father came from a very big family, and a very poor one, in Minnesota. My mother was an early daughter of divorce. She had to quit college to help raise her siblings. Both of them thought, Hey, without the younger siblings I had to take care of, I might have pursued a different life." Falbo, therefore, found herself growing up without brothers or sisters. So when she got to the University of California at Los Angeles as a graduate student in psychology, she decided to study only children. "It was the early 1970s, and what we were all interested in was stereotypes. Stereotypes about men and women especially, and also

blacks and whites. It struck me that one of the small stereotypes in our culture was about only children."

In an earlier day, she says, that prejudice was understand-
able: "If you want your ethnic or religious group to prosper,
you need large numbers. And if you have fifty percent mortality, you need a big base rate. If you just had one kid, you were
underachieving." In the empty, agricultural United States of
the nineteenth century, "the more kids the better." And in the
first part of the twentieth century, as efficiency experts like the
father in *Cheaper by the Dozen* came to the fore, "mass production really permeated the American culture." But by the
1970s, with the publication of books such as *The Population
Bomb*, more children didn't necessarily seem better to Falbo.
"My gut sense when I began was that these kids were not as
bad as people said. After all, I was an only child."[43]

Trained in experimental psychology, she set the stereotype
as her hypotheses: "only children are selfish"; "only children
are spoiled." And then she set out to prove them. "We used
typical college student populations, gave them paper-and-
pencil questionnaires." It didn't take long to sense that the
stereotypes didn't hold up very well—that they were seeing a
lot of ordinary onlies. Meanwhile, Falbo and colleagues began
the long process of examining all the other studies done since
the 1920s on only children. These studies tended to be small,
obscure—"you'd get a Canadian mental health center, a German clinic for nailbiting"—and they'd been mostly ignored.
But by the mid-1980s, with her colleague Denise Polit, Falbo
was ready to publish a review of all the data she'd been able to
find, 141 studies in all. They'd covered every aspect of "personality development" from self-esteem and autonomy to maturity, generosity to contentment, peer popularity to relations
with parents. And they found—this is pretty much the punch

line to this chapter—that *"only children scored significantly better than other groups in achievement motivation and personal adjustment"* and were in all other respects indistinguishable from children with brothers and sisters.[44]

As interesting as their findings was their reasoning. Earlier researchers, still under the spell of G. Stanley Hall, had expected to find problems with only kids and hence their hypotheses revolved around "sibling deprivation." The unusual thing, that is, about only children was that they lacked brothers or sisters. But by the time they'd examined all the studies, Falbo and Polit concluded "the most parsimonious" explanation for these kids' success was something they *did* have—undivided parental attention. "Because only children receive more attention from their parents, they are likely to exhibit more 'character' than other children, character here consisting of such traits as maturity and cooperativeness." And since they spend more time "under the concentrated surveillance of their parents, we argue that they are more likely to develop a sense of personal control than other children. Personal control means here the belief that one has control over one's life outcomes." It was all in the language of social scientists—a meta-analysis of independent variables, with endless discussion of "parental attention mechanisms" and weighted samples and statistical significances. But drily, patiently, methodically, it finally demolished—for anyone who happened to be reading the *Journal of Marriage and the Family*—those stories about the DEFT and the STOUT and the BIRTHMARKED and the CRUEL. As the authors noted in their final summation, "These findings contradict the notion that a country populated with substantial proportions of only children would be a country whose character would be substantially altered."[45]

Their data also fit with a burst of other studies on more

limited aspects of the life of only children that have appeared in the last two decades. Pretty much any worry a parent might suggest has been looked into.

Are only children lonely? Not really; studies of undergraduates show only children have the same number of friends, and report feeling no lonelier.[46] In fact, one psychologist suggests that children from small families seem to feel more "urgency" about finding outside playmates, while the data shows youngsters from large families can be "more parochial and limited in their understanding of a variety of social roles."[47]

Are only children unpopular with their peers? That's been studied too—when teachers chart who is chosen first when kids are picking sides for a game, only children are the most frequently chosen.[48]

Are they shy, unable to stand up for themselves? Not really, perhaps because they now have plenty of chances to grow up with other children, even if they're not in the same house. "In day care and nursery school, young children learn how to compete, how to share," said one psychologist. "These preschool lessons accomplish the same things as interaction with siblings. Nursery school isn't 24 hours a day, but six hours is enough to learn how to get along with other children."[49]

Are they *spoiled*? This is what we really want to know—if there's any stereotype that sticks in almost everyone's mind, this is it. A huge pile of presents under the Christmas tree—all for him! The little prince! It's a little hard to tell, of course, since we live in a culture where almost everyone is at least a little spoiled, where spoiling children underwrites a significant part of the economy. In my house, even though there's no TV pushing products, there's nonetheless an irreducible rubble of books, blocks, trucks, cars, dolls, and stuffed animals—they seem to generate spontaneously. So the real question is, are only children spoiled *rotten*. Are they made *extra* selfish by the extra attention that comes their way?

The studies seem to show that the answer is no; different researchers report "either that there are no differences by number of siblings, or that the differences favor the only child," according to Judith Blake.[50] She speculates that the spoiled only child is a myth spread by parents in large families, who tell their children when they complain about a lack of privacy that conditions in small families spoil children, making them self-centered and aloof. "Since so many more people come from large families rather than small ones, it's not too surprising that prejudices against small families have been widely transmitted."[51]

In fact, you could argue that it's easier for children to share if they don't spend their entire lives in constant battles for parental attention. A kindergarten teacher told one re-searcher: "It's the ones who have been jostled and have had to compete who are always trying to push someone down, to be first in line, or yell louder in order to be heard. Onlies have always been heard and therefore function in a very calm way. They are very easy to deal with in a group because they feel confident that their turn will come because it always has. . . . When they come in at the beginning of the kindergarten year, they are really modelling very good behavior for the others."[52] This squares emotionally with my experience. My life as a (not very nice) older brother didn't teach me much about sharing; it taught me a good deal about how to jockey for everything from the biggest helping of pot roast to the biggest dollop of praise. I had a hard time sharing the *back seat of the car*. I'm glad I had a brother, but I somehow managed to end up spoiled nonetheless.

People lodge other complaints against the possibility of only children. "They'll be too mature," some say, as if this was really something to fear. It's true that only children deal more easily witn adults because they spend more time at it; but this is a society where adolescents get pregnant, take drugs, *die* because they haven't matured. Whatever maturity represents, say the researchers, it's not something that plagues only kids— they score slightly better on an "anomie index" (questions measuring the feeling the world is uncaring, "going to the dogs") and a resentment index (feelings of being cheated, getting a "raw deal").[53]

Only children may have some other real bonuses in their lives, too. Several studies suggest that singletons have more flexible sex-role orientation, which is to say that researchers find boys playing with dolls and girls with trucks. Some speculate it's because their parents make up for only having a boy or a girl by letting the child develop positive traits of both genders. "The professionally successful daughter or the emotionally nurturant son could sufficiently satisfy the needs of both parents in a way that might reduce the need for gender diversity."[54] This effect seems particularly pronounced for girls, perhaps because more parents continue to hope for a boy than a girl, and so if they have an only daughter tend to raise her as a tomboy.

In the effort to study sociability, researchers have investigated everything from basketball teams to hunting licenses. Differences between kids are slight, but only children are more likely to be involved in extracurricular activities in general, in clubs and hobbies, and in acting, singing, and dancing. They take more pictures, play more music, raise more animals, and collect more stamps than non–only children, who play more sports, especially on teams, hunt and fish more often, and do more woodworking and cooking. Even when socioeconomic status has been factored out, only children show more interest in science, music, math, and literature, while kids with siblings care more for office, mechanical, and technical work, skilled trades, and labor. (They were equally interested in sales, whatever that means.)[55] One researcher compiled the lovely-sounding Index of Richness of Past Experience, and discovered that onlies were more likely to have danced, smoked, sent an entry blank to a contest, ridden a pony, ridden on a merry-go-round, and cashed a check.[56]

But what, you ask, about self-esteem, the chief goal of any self-respecting modern? Here, it must be reported, onlies fall somewhere in the middle of the pack. Firstborn children have the highest sense of themselves, because, say researchers, "they are generally more capable, larger, and more skilled than their siblings," and so come to regard themselves more favorably. Lastborns, being smaller than everyone else and unable to do as much, develop the least self-esteem. Middleborns and only children score about the same, but for different reasons. Middleborns are bigger than some of their siblings and smaller than others; hence, so are their egos. "In contrast, only children do not experience a sibling comparison, and consequently their self-esteem development is unaffected by the comparison process." They're simply who they are. And in any event, they seem to be functioning—at least three studies indicate that only children are underrepresented among psychiatric or other clinical clients.[57]

Only children end up marrying at the same age as everyone else, and their divorce rate is no higher than anyone else's (which, admittedly, isn't saying much).[58] Even their politics have been studied. To judge from the fifty-two singletons who served in Congress from 1981 to 1983, and the fifty-six who

served between 1985 and 1987, they are identical to politicians as a whole—no more or less favorable to the MX missile,
equally likely to support solar energy, indistinguishable in
their attitudes toward the contras, neutron bombs, clean air,
due process, abortion, and "nerve gas development."[59]

What's most telling about this tidal wave of research is that
it often measures the childhoods of an earlier age—the 1950s,
the 1960s, or, in the case of some of the congressmen, the
1920s. If you were going to find any huge differences between
only kids and kids with siblings, it would have been back then,
before the spread of day care and preschool, before almost
every child had a social calendar as thick as a Parisian debu-
tante's. "For G. Stanley Hall, growing up in rural New England, running around and playing all the time *was*
childhood," says Falbo. "And who would you play with, how
would you learn to interact, if you didn't have siblings?
Women of the class he was interested in didn't work, and
maybe he was right to think that it wasn't healthy for a kid to
be stuck with her alone all day, to be overprotected and
overindulged. You can see it. But look at now. Most mothers
of young children are working—they can't be overprotecting
them because they hardly get to see them. Most kids are in
some kind of day care. Very early on they have plenty of peer
experience."

Only children, in other words, are no worse than any
other kids. On most measures of achievement and personality,
they score slightly better than other children, but the emphasis should be on "slightly." "When you can find differences,"
says Falbo, "it's no more than a two percent difference. It only
shows up when you examine very large numbers. You can't sit
on an airplane and tell whether the person in the next seat is
an only."

Falbo sits back on her chair, sips her drink, sighs. "I tell you, I've done this research up one side and down the other. Believe me, my career would have taken off—it would have been Nobel Prize stuff—if I'd found that only kids were sick, sick, sick. They're not. The conventional wisdom is wrong. But this still hasn't sunk in."

chapter
two

Beijing—It was just another school day for Liu
Huamin when the father of one of her students
burst through the classroom door and said his
teen-age son was threatening to commit suicide
by jumping off the fourth-floor balcony of the
family's apartment building.

Why? asked Mrs. Liu, a chemistry teacher at
Waluji Middle School.

Because, the man replied, the boy's mother
would not cook his favorite meat dumplings for
breakfast.

Whoa! File that boy under GLUTTONY. And according to
New York Times reporter Patrick Tyler, he's not alone.

Indeed, it seems at times as if the willfulness of China's generation of "little emperors"—children growing up without

siblings under China's one-child population control policy—knows no bounds.

In Guangdong Province a power failure prevented a housewife from cooking dinner for her 14-year-old son, who flew into a rage and went out to watch television with a friend. When the boy returned there was still no dinner, so he seized a meat cleaver and killed his mother with ten blows to the head. Then he hanged himself.

If I want to show definitively that only children are as healthy as any others, if I want to drive a stake through the heart of this prejudice, then there's no way around considering China, the nation with by far the world's largest population of only children, as well as the source of some of the most potent images of their wickedness. For the time being, let's disregard the question of whether the country's one-child policy is a good idea or not. (I think it's a draconian mess, a perhaps unnecessary bureaucratic abuse that I'll discuss later in this book.) For now, consider just the children that have resulted from the edict. There's a remarkable unity of opinion about them in the West, not just among right-to-lifers, but among virtually everyone else—the opinion is every bit as unanimous as it was in this country in the decades following G. Stanley Hall's pronouncements.

In fact, the stories sound an awful lot like those early personality profiles from the *Pedagogical Seminary*. The dumpling suicide was, admitted *Times* reporter Tyler, "an extreme case" (and thank heaven for that), but it "illustrates the concern of many Chinese that its first generation of only children is rapidly maturing into a generation of spoiled, self-absorbed tyrants." Social scientists no longer collect cabinets of the Peculiar and Exceptional, and it wouldn't make much difference if they did, for their journals are not widely read. But reporters have no hope of studying a real sample of 1.2 billion Chinese to determine if there's really a problem with only children. They have a few days, a hypothesis, and a collection of anecdotes and experts. So it's unfair to pick on Tyler, but I do want to dissect his account, because it makes clear how stereotypes play in our heads.

Almost immediately after telling his horror stories, Tyler shifts his article in a different direction. Though he never says so, we stop hearing about *only* children, and we start hearing about *pampered* children, about whether parents who grew up "in troubled and violent times under Mao, suffering long periods of deprivation in the countryside and interrupted schooling," are now overcompensating by giving their kids too much. "The current generation of parents has been cut adrift from both the traditional Confucian values emphasizing reverence for elders, and from the Communist values imposed for three decades under Mao," Tyler reports. Therefore, say "specialists," it is too early to tell whether these little emperors will grow to "be a generation of self-centered autocrats, whose politics may be more aggressive than the generation that grew up under Mao, or whether they are so overindulged at home that they will be ill-prepared for the competitive pressures and harsh realities of China's market economy." Either way, disaster looms. "We teachers often wonder how these students can take up their social responsibility when they get older," says Mrs. Liu, the chemistry teacher.

And what is the proof? Well, their parents are spending more money than ever before on "toys, books, educational materials, personal computers, and food." One Johns Hopkins anthropologist met a woman who "took her daughter to McDonald's twice a week to give her modern nutrition." Not only that, "one of China's most popular amusement parks, 'Windows on the World,' has no rides and no arcades. Chinese come from all over the country to pay, in some cases a week's wages, to show their children miniatures of Manhattan Island, the Statue of Liberty, the Eiffel Tower, and the Taj Mahal." Sort of like spending a week's wages to take the family *(from all over America they come!)* to Disney World, no? I hear they have a miniature Leaning Tower of Pisa there.

"Most of our time and money are spent on this child," said Wen Geli, the mother of a 2-year-old boy who seems less attentive to the park's attractions than to gorging himself on ice cream. "We want to give him an introduction to the world and expand his outlook." . . .

Not far away, a retired sports teacher, Cai Kunling, 59, was squiring his 5-year-old granddaughter, Fu Hua, past the wonders of the world. "She should be in kindergarten today," he said, "but she wanted to take me to this place," he added in a tone that reflected who was in charge.

The two of them sat for their photo in front of a miniature of Niagara Falls and then strolled over to the little Manhattan.

To Mr. Cai, who lived through the Mao period, it was like a dream world.

"My generation made a lot of sacrifices and had a lot of devotion to the country," he said. "But this generation needs a reward if you want them to do something. If there is no compensation, they don't want to do it."

But isn't that the point? Didn't we want the Chinese to stop "making a lot of sacrifices" for Mao? Wasn't the Cultural Revolution supposed to be a *bad thing?* Why, to quote from the

Harvard expert interviewed by Tyler, should anyone be concerned if the next generation is "going to be able to 'eat bitterness,' to sacrifice themselves as was true under socialism"?[1]

And what does any of this have to do with only children, anyway?

And why did no one talk to Toni Falbo, who, as it happens, has some actual data on this issue?

A few blocks from the hotel where the Population Association held its meeting, the National Gallery of Art had mounted "The Splendors of Imperial China." Falbo and I stood in front of a gorgeously detailed sixteenth-century hand scroll showing *The Imperial Procession to the Ming Mausoleums*, and she talked about her work, with both Chinese and American colleagues, in China. "It was relatively easy to get permission to do research there since I was a foreigner, and they knew the results wouldn't necessarily be published inside China," she said. They picked a thousand subjects, third- and sixth-graders from four provinces. They weighed them, gave them math and verbal tests, and then gave parents, teachers, peers, and the children themselves a set of questionnaires to fill out. "If everyone else said these kids were fine, and the only kids themselves said they were miserable, that would be interesting," explains Falbo. "If the teachers thought they were difficult, that would be interesting. If the parents thought they were losers, that would be interesting. If their peers thought they were spoiled, that would be interesting."[2] And the result? Nothing interesting.

Just like American only children, the Chinese little emperors did slightly better in school. They were slightly healthier. And their personalities were mostly indistinguishable from those of their peers. In Gansu, one of the four provinces, "only children received lower evaluations from their parents" than kids from big families, a finding the researchers described as "curious since teachers, peers, and the children themselves did not regard the same children" as problematic.[3] Falbo and her colleagues also conducted a major study in the urban and rural areas of Changchun, an industrial area in Jilin Province in northeastern China that is sometimes referred to as the country's Detroit and Hollywood combined because of its large car factories and movie studios. There, working with local researchers, they tested for what the Chinese called "virtue," a constellation of personality attributes that include respect and stoicism. "Only children do not appear to differ from children with siblings."[4] It's all rather dull.

So why are so many Chinese, and so many newspaper reporters, convinced the country is poised for a wave of meat-cleaver attacks? Probably, says Falbo, because of a statistical problem uncovered in 1969 by social scientists in this country. They were studying the question of birth order, and trying to figure out why there was such a high percentage of firstborn children showing up in samples of everything from National Merit Scholars to striptease artists. The answer turned out to be simple. In the early years of the baby boom, between 1947 and 1950, an enormous number of new families were started; the babies born in that period were much more likely to be firstborns. So when you measured National Merit Scholars nineteen years later, it was no wonder they were overrepresented. Now the Chinese make the same mistake. If 30 percent of high school students threatening to jump off roofs because their mothers won't make them dumplings are only children, that sounds like proof of something—unless it turns out that 30 percent of their classmates are also only children, in which case you better look for your answer elsewhere. Perhaps that two-year-old was less attentive to the miniature

Statue of Liberty than to "gorging himself on ice cream" because he was two, not because he lacked a brother. "If American psychiatrists go over there and look at a class of only kids, they look normal to them," says Falbo. "They don't want to do things they don't want to do, they like chocolate cake. Hey, they're normal. But before, kids were so obedient, sometimes because they were so malnourished, that these kids seem different. It's not an only kid thing—it's a changing world. If a family has enough money to have three kids, they have three little emperors. They buy them all computers and piano lessons."[5]

• • • •

So stereotypes derive from lazy thinking. And also from wishful thinking—in the endless modern effort to "get in touch" with ourselves, we cling to the notion that things like the number of our siblings determine our personality. (Not as hard as we cling to, say, astrology, but pretty hard nonetheless.) After all, we're all somebody's children: here's something that can explain *us*.

Just two years ago an MIT researcher named Frank Sulloway published a book on birth order called *Born to Rebel* that became a best-seller despite many hundreds of pages filled with graphs and charts. In fact, those graphs and charts pretty much overwhelmed many of the reviewers. Writing in *The New Yorker*, Robert Boynton described the book as "a sophisticated multivariate analysis of 3,890 scientists who took part in 28 scientific revolutions; the 893 members of the National Convention that ruled France during the French Revolution; 700 men and women who were involved in the Protestant Reformation; and participants in 61 American reform movements." These people yielded "more than a million biographical data points culled from 500 years of history," compiled by an author who in twenty-six years "read 20,000 biographies." Allowing for weekends, that's 2.958 biographies a day, which *is* pretty impressive, especially since "entering the data in a computer took two years, and designing the book's graphs took another year."[6]

Sulloway's basic finding: firstborns are much more likely to resist scientific and social revolutions, while laterborns are natural rebels, inclined to identify with the underdogs. That's because kids compete for the limited affection and attention of their parents in a Darwinian effort to increase their chances of survival. Firstborns, "having grabbed parental attention when they had a monopoly," do everything they can to hold on to it. Laterborns, desperately seeking a way to break open that tight bond, become extremely inventive. "Individual temperament is thus shaped by birth order. It stands to reason that firstborns will be conservative, since already existing niches most benefit them. For laterborns, by contrast, the alternative is innovation or obscurity. No wonder that Voltaire, a younger brother, became a leading figure of the Enlightenment, while Armand, his firstborn brother, became a religious fanatic." No wonder that during the first decades of the Copernican revolution, laterborns were five times as likely as firstborns to accept the theory that the earth rotates around the sun. Birth order, Sulloway believes, "provides a potential Rosetta stone"; in the words of one reviewer, he credits his computer printouts with "resolving debates that have characterized the study of human beings since Machiavelli and Hobbes. There really is such a thing as human nature, and birth order determines it."[7]

Most people never got around to reading the book, of course, but they could get plenty of pleasure from the lists that appeared in every article about it. Charles Darwin was a laterborn, as were Ben Franklin and Bill Gates. Franklin D. Roosevelt, Winston Churchill, Joseph Stalin, *and* Marcia Clark were firstborns. Also Courtney Love, Mao Tse-tung, and Margaret Mead. Not Madonna—she came late to her family, as did Joan of Arc, Marx, Lenin, and Jefferson, Ross Perot, Katie Couric, Mahatma Gandhi, and—get this—not only John Candy but George Carlin, Eddie Murphy, and Billy Crystal. George Washington, however, was a firstborn, as was Rush Limbaugh.

Once the initial buzz about the book died down, some critics noted that Sulloway always seemed willing to make exceptions for people who didn't fit his rules. Napoleon, it was pointed out, was a laterborn, and yet he became an autocrat—if the eldest sibling happens to be "a wimp," that can happen, said Sulloway.[8] And a series of extended reviews, especially in academic journals, punched serious holes in his argument. One of the cleverest attacks came from Alan Wolfe in *The New Republic,* employing a variant of the argument about why firstborns showed up among National Merit Scholars in 1969. Revolutionary times, he maintained, have their own dynamic. "In such times laterborns will be more radical for no other reason than that they were born later. I was 26 in 1968 and considered myself quite radical, but it was obvious to me that those born just a few years later than myself were even more radical."[9] The very intensity of revolutionary eras, in other words, might explain why younger siblings are more radical; it is their youth, not their birth order. The older brother works for Dr. King and his kid sister works for black power not because they competed for attention with their parents but because they came of age five years apart—and in a revolution, five years is an eternity.

For understanding only children, though, Sulloway's methodology can stand or fall; he can be a prophet or a fraud. Because it turns out that an only child is not an autocratic firstborn or a rebellious laterborn—she's her own girl. Sulloway theorizes that she may be a little more conservative than not (after all, there's always the potential threat of another sibling), but his data shows only children to be "the least predictable subgroup in any family dynamics model, precisely because they have no siblings."[10] There's no kid brother to fill the rebel niche, no older sister to rule the roost. Even if a nation like China wanted to "reduce ideological disparities" by prohibiting more than one child, writes Sulloway, it wouldn't work—"singletons tend to be more variable."[11] Their political and religious attitudes fall almost exactly between his firstborns and lastborns; onlies vary significantly, according to his numbers, on openness to scientific innovation, the number of scientific interests, liberal social attitudes, and amount of world travel, all of which combine to form his Index of Openness to Experience.[12] They are, in other words, the wild cards.

Perhaps you would like a list. Elvis Presley was an only child, also Leonardo da Vinci, Nancy Reagan, Robin Williams, Brooke Shields, Joe Montana, and Jean-Paul Sartre. The *Los Angeles Times*, in its story on Sulloway's book, originally identified Lucille Ball as an only child, but alert readers pointed out that in fact she had a younger brother. There is no question about John Updike, Chelsea Clinton, Hans Christian Andersen, Lauren Bacall, Charles Lindbergh, Indira Gandhi, or Dr. Ruth Westheimer. Three onlies—Frank Borman, William Anders, and James Lovell, Jr.—comprised the first Apollo crew to orbit the moon in 1968, perhaps because NASA, along with looking for short test pilots, was also interested in finding only children for its original missions. "They reckoned that having grown up alone you might tolerate being alone in a space capsule better," says Falbo. "That seems like a jump to me."[13]

•　　•　　•

I said at the beginning of this book that the issue of only children is nowhere near as sensitive as race or gender. But it is nonetheless emotionally charged for most of us, sensitive enough that we're happy to stick to stereotypes instead of thinking it through. That's because 80 percent of us grew up with siblings[14]—to imagine having only one child is to imagine what it would have been like if our parents had made the same choice, which may well leave you feeling sad or disloyal or selfish. (Or, if you're a younger sibling, nonexistent.) It's a loaded topic. You've known your sister far longer than your wife; your brother will be there after your parents are dead; you've gone through bitternesses and traumas with them that would have wrecked any normal friendship.

For all that, psychologists and social scientists know very little about the roles that siblings play in our lives. Traditionally, they've been seen as "very minor actors on the stage of human development," says Stephen Bank, the Wesleyan University psychiatrist who coauthored *The Sibling Bond* with Michael Kahn.[15] "We were usually able to respond intelligently to our patients, in individual and family psychotherapy, when they discussed the bonds between parents and children or those between husbands and wives. But we found ourselves poorly prepared to understand and connect with what our patients were saying when they spoke of their feelings about brothers and sisters whose emotional presence still cast a shadow over their lives." You can marry your spouse, and you can divorce him; you can grow out of certain relations with your parents—that's why we have various rituals to mark our "coming of age." But not with brothers and sisters— they're just *there*.

"When we tried to exercise our skills as psychologists in the emotional, and largely irrational, realm of sibling relations, we felt as if we were in a foreign country without a map," write Bank and Kahn.[16] They began to pay much closer attention to what they were hearing about brothers and sisters, "making copious notes whenever an individual patient or a family member expressed distress about a relationship with a sibling." They heard stories about three sisters trying to decide whether to place their ailing mother in a nursing home—the eldest and the youngest wanted the middle sister, who was always favored by the mother, to make the choice (and pay the bill); about a ten-year-old boy who began to speak about suicide after his younger brother was killed by a car and six weeks later had a serious bicycle accident, landing him in the same hospital where his brother had died; about a man who neglected his marriage and his job as he "overinvolved" himself with his emotionally disturbed brother; about a thirteen-year-old boy brutally beaten by his delinquent older brother who told a therapist he didn't fight back because his older brother was his idol; about two children, ages three and five, who preferred one another to the total exclusion of other kids.

"Our patients' reactions to being asked about their brothers and sisters were astonishing. In response to the right questions, many people suddenly developed insights into sources of their self-defeating patterns and came away feeling more able to cope with problems. . . . Others became so defensive that we (and they) knew a sensitive area had been hit."[17]

One thing their research soon showed, in fact, was that siblings are most likely to form strong bonds when they've "been deprived of reliable parental care." When people have "emotionally fulfilling" ties to their parents—or to their own spouses or children—then "the sibling bond will be weaker and less important." Your sister can be, in other words, a kind of fallback mechanism, a relationship of last resort. And that relationship can be "helpful or harmful, depending on the circumstances of each family, the personalities of the children, and the actions and attitudes of the parents."[18]

We all know about the helpful side—if we haven't experienced it ourselves, we've seen it in a thousand sitcoms. Greg may have teased Marcia, but he was always there for her in the end when she colored her hair bright green. Penn State psychologist Judy Dunn has shown that the arrival of a brother or sister gives both kids the opportunity to learn social skills like empathizing with another person, making jokes, resolving arguments. Toddlers as young as fourteen months miss their older siblings when they're absent; often a brother or sister (and no one else) can comfort a crying baby if the mother or father is away.[19] Even fighting with their siblings can help kids, just as it helps all other young primates: "Aggression, even when painful, represents contact, warmth, another presence. . . . Sibling aggression has a reassuringly predictable quality: if one punches or insults a sibling in a predictable way, the retort, though painful, is familiar and expected."[20] (I hope my brother felt this way about it.)

We talk less frequently about the problems siblings cause each other. Even the term we use for such discussions, "sibling rivalry," sounds fairly tame—we might be talking about the Red Sox and the Yankees, engaged in a high-spirited contest with handshakes all around after the final out. But in fact, it can be a pretty bitter lifelong contest. One study showed that laterborn kids, before they even turned three, behaved less assertively and positively toward peers than only kids—"laterborns were thought to develop an aversion to others" because they had been victims of "undesirable sibling interactions."[21]

For the older child, having a new baby brother or sister can be joyful; and when it's a struggle, when he feels displaced, it can build character, "the occasion for helping a child strengthen himself and become more, not less."[22] But it can be truly painful, too, and for all concerned. In one study researchers watched mothers play with their oldest child a few months prior to the delivery of a second child, and then again several weeks after the delivery. "Each mother's emotional response to her eldest had changed dramatically: she was 'emotionally flat' and less interested, and her reactions were forced and labored."[23] It's like the kind of sternness you need to break off any love affair; inside, you're probably crying, but the die is cast.

Parents often view a second child as a gift for the first, but ironically it's precisely those olderborns who have the most "playful, intense" relationships with their mothers that treat their new siblings with the most hostility—and whose younger brothers and sisters are most hostile to *them* before they even reach their first birthday.[24] Describing a series of "poignant" laboratory observations, two researchers found that "it is not uncommon for a one-to-two-year-old sibling to approach repeatedly an irritated older sibling with attempts to start joint play or with 'helpful' overtures, only to be rebuffed time and time again, often with physical force."[25]

Sometimes the hurts go on forever: Bank and Kahn tell the story of a chronically unhappy older sister who feels perpetually anxious and driven and cannot understand why she and her sister still don't get along.[26] And sometimes the hurts are very deep. Sibling incest has been estimated to be at least five times as frequent as parent-child incest, and many researchers think that's an underestimate; Bank and Kahn say its "greater frequency does not mean that its ramifications are any less significant" than parent-child incest. It's not "child's play"—it has "profound implications for personality development."[27]

• • •

Siblings are often wildly different, one from another—on average their IQs are 14 points apart, for instance, compared with a mere 6 points between social classes.[28] How could that be, given that siblings share not only genes but also parents, home environments, neighborhoods, educational backgrounds? The same station is playing on the radio, whether it's NPR or Howard Stern; the same food is on the table, whether it's organic vegetarian or Happy Meals; the parents are giving each other the same number of hugs or black eyes. So why on earth are siblings often so different?

When psychologists Judy Dunn and Robert Plomin set out to answer that question in their book *Separate Lives*, they began with literature, looking for clues in what authors had written about their childhoods. Dickens, of course, faced all sorts of hardship and poverty as a boy, but the incident that really stuck in his mind concerned his older sister Fanny. When he was twelve, and had been sent off to work in a factory, she won a scholarship to the Royal Academy of Music and a silver medal from Princess Augusta. "The tears ran down my face," he said, not tears of happiness for her success, but bitter tears at seeing his parents' pride in her success. "I prayed, when I went to bed that night, to be lifted out of the humiliation and neglect in which I was. I never had suffered so much before." And indeed, he would later write in *Great Expectations:* "In the little world in which children have their existence, whosoever brings them up, there is nothing so finely perceived, and so finely felt, as injustice."[29]

In other words, there is one difference between the lives of siblings: how they think their parents are treating them. This "hypersensitivity" drives much of psychological development, according to Dunn and Plomin.[30] Or, as Tommy Smothers put it to his brother night after night, "Mom always loved you best." Very often, a mother *does* love one child best, a subject so painful that we had best retreat to numbers in discussing it. In a Colorado study only a third of mothers reported feeling "a similar intensity and extent of affection" for both of their children, and only a third said they gave similar attention to both. Fifty-two percent said they felt more affection toward their younger child, and only 13 percent toward the older; in a similar study in Cambridge, England, 61 percent liked their younger child better and only 10 percent their firstborn.[31] These numbers surprise me; they don't seem to describe most of the mothers I know. Perhaps they are dated; perhaps the favoritism is just a temporary phenomenon. But children seem to feel it—two-thirds of five- and six-year-olds told researchers that their mother favored either them or their sibling,[32] and most of the firstborns thought she liked the baby best.[33] And even when parents have no favorite, of course, it often seems they do. You have to cuddle one-year-olds, and you have to sometimes take a stern line with a four-year-old. Even if the four-year-old was cuddled when *she* was one, what she sees every day is the difference—in tone of voice, in attention, in *delight*. The baby has learned a new word! How adorable. The kindergartner has learned a new word, too: "Poophead." And according to Dunn and Plomin, "seeing your mother's evident affection for your sibling may override any amount of affection you in fact receive."[34] These differences "contribute significantly" to problem behaviors and depressed moods in a sample of seven-year-olds, and they can last a lifetime. One study found marked preferences among elderly parents of adult children.[35] In the immortal words of poet Philip Larkin:

They fuck you up, your mum and dad.
They may not mean to, but they do.[36]

It's not that parents of only children can't figure out a thousand ways to screw up their children's lives as well. I've managed to be, at various times, too distant, too stern, and too adult, and I'm sure that Sophie bears the marks of each, as well as of a dozen other mistakes that I've made along the way. But when parents of only children need to console themselves for not having given their child a brother or a sister, they can at least know that this differential affection is one category of powerful mistake from which they're exempt.

And the parents of only children *will* need to console themselves from time to time. Even if their child fits the norm and turns out fine—not SPOILED, not GLUTTONOUS; even if she gets into a good college and finds a good job and marries a good person and has a good child of her own; even then her parents will still be stuck with the profound fear that she will be left alone at the end of her life.

And to that fear there is no pat or easy answer, no comforting study. "The diminution of family size makes one potentially more vulnerable at the end of life," in the words of therapists Bank and Kahn, "without the main human connection between past and present."[37] There's no one else with whom you share as much of your history—as many birthdays and reunions and baby showers. No one else with whom you shared *parents*. It's true that painful relationships with your siblings, and the pathologies they breed, can last a lifetime, too, but those are not the scenes we wish or imagine for our children. It was, perhaps, the hardest part of the decision we made about stopping at a single child—the idea that at the end of Sophie's life she may be lonely in a special way. (And the selfish idea that she may not be completely able to remember *me* because she has no one to remember me *with*.) As Nicholas

Eberstadt points out in a recent article in *The Public Interest,* in a world with many only children "'family' would be understood as a unit that does not include any biological contemporaries or peers."[38] There is no use pretending that won't be wrenching, and often sad.

•   •   •

So many things affect how many kids we decide to have: the cost, for instance (currently it will run you $249,556 to raise a kid to eighteen, more if you live in the urban West, not including college),[39] or the fact that most women now work, or the boom in divorces.

More people are choosing to have a single child. But they're likely doing it for such pragmatic reasons, because the folklore that surrounds only children hasn't faded much from the turn of the last century. In the popular mind, G. Stanley Hall still reigns. Given a choice between childlessness and a single child, for instance, undergraduates in one poll preferred having no kids at all—by a six-to-one margin.[40] Grandparents still nag, and neighbors, too. The advice columnists still promise disaster: George Crane, author of *The Worry Clinic,* declared that onlies are more rigid in their political views, more irritable, more likely to divorce—and that parents should therefore have at least three kids. Niki Scott, author of the syndicated "Working Woman" column, used virtually the same words as those early studies—only children were at great risk of becoming "miniature adults."[41]

But by now such charges should bounce off you. I am well aware that this book may not persuade most readers to limit themselves to one child—there are many deep factors involved in that decision. But I do hope that it at least helps end this particular prejudice. It's simply not true; only kids aren't different from anyone else.

I've just come in from raising the seat on my daughter's bike. One minute she was in tears because she'd lost her new bike helmet; a minute later she was careening down the driveway yelling at the dog to follow her. She's not an only kid— she's a kid. That's the news.

PART TWO

SPECIES

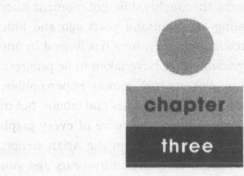

chapter

three

BEWARE OF PEOPLE PREACHING THAT WE LIVE IN SPECIAL TIMES.
PEOPLE HAVE PREACHED THAT MESSAGE BEFORE, AND THOSE
who listened sold their furniture and climbed up on rooftops
awaiting ascension, or built boats to float out the coming
flood, or laced up their Nikes and swallowed poison in some
California subdivision. These are the prophets with visions of
the seven-headed Beast, with a taste for the hairshirt and the
scourge, with twirling eyes. No, better by far to listen to Ecclesiastes, the original wise preacher, jaded from a thousand mes-
siahs and a thousand revivals:

> One generation passes away, and another generation comes;
> but the earth abides forever.... That which has been is
> what will be, that which is done is what will be done, and
> there is nothing new under the sun. Is there anything of
> which it may be said, "See, this is new?" It has already been
> in ancient times before us.[1]

And yet, for all that, we may live in a special time. We may live in the strangest, most thoroughly different moment since humans took up farming ten thousand years ago and time more or less commenced. Since then time has flowed in one direction—toward *more*, which we have taken to be progress. At first the momentum was gradual, almost imperceptible, checked by wars and dark ages and plagues and taboos; but in recent centuries it has accelerated, the curve of every graph steepening like the Himalayas rising from the Asian steppe. We have climbed quite high. Of course, fifty years ago you could have said the same thing, and fifty years before that, and fifty years before *that*. But if you had, you would have been premature, too hasty. Our population has grown four times larger in that 150 years; our harvests have grown much faster than that; the size of our economies has doubled again and again and again.

But now—now may be the special time. So special that in the western world we might each of us consider, among many other things, reproducing at a rate as low as human beings have ever voluntarily reproduced. I've shown, I think, that single-child families can work; now we need to see if they're necessary. We need to see if we're finally running up against some limits.

• • •

Not far from the office where I used to work in Midtown Manhattan, a storefront window offered passersby a look at a "population clock," a kind of human odometer relentlessly tallying our growing numbers. The ever-increasing total looked ominous—about 3 new people each second,[2] 10,000 an hour, a quarter million a day.[3] Since the mid-1960s, we've lived with the idea that there is a "population bomb" or a "population explosion" or, at the very least, a "population crisis." If children of a slightly earlier generation expected to end up buried beneath radioactive debris, children of my generation expected in somewhat the same unspoken way that eventually people would stand shoulder to shoulder on their own few feet of land in a desperately overcrowded world.

To figure out if we're nearing certain limits, the first question you need to ask is, *how many of us are there?* So here is the first piece of news that may alter the way you see the planet, the first indication we live at a special moment. Oddly enough, it is, at least at first blush, a hopeful indicator: *new demographic evidence shows that it is at least possible that a child born today will live long enough to see the peak of human population.*

Around the world people are choosing to have fewer and fewer children—not just in China where the government forces it on them, but in almost every nation outside the poorest parts of Africa. Population growth rates are lower than at any time since World War II;[4] in the last three decades, excluding China, the average woman in the developing world has gone from bearing six children to bearing four.[5] Even in Bangladesh the average has fallen from six to less than four; even in the mullahs' Iran it's dropped by three full children.[6] If this keeps up, the population of the world will not quite double again—the United Nations guesses it will top out at between 10 and 11 billion, up from just under 6 billion at the moment, and the peak could be even lower.[7] The world is still growing, growing at nearly a record pace: we add a New York City every month, nearly a Mexico every year, almost an India each decade. But we may be over the top of the roller-coaster—that growth is no longer "exponential," "unstoppable," "inexorable," "unchecked," "cancerous." If current trends hold, population growth will all but end before the twenty-first century is out.

And that will be none too soon; there is no way we could keep going as we have been. The *increase* in human population in the 1990s exceeds the *total* population in 1600.[8] There has been more population growth since 1950 than during the previous 4 million years.[9] Demographers—described by one of their tribe as people "with a flair for numbers who lack the personality to become accountants"[10]—love to play statistical games with these rapid rates: if population kept growing at its current pace for a mere 6,500 years, "the descendants of the present world population would form a solid sphere of live bodies expanding with a radial velocity that, neglecting relativity, would equal the velocity of light."[11]

The reasons for our recent rapid growth are pretty clear. For most of human history it took more than a millennium for population to double; the Industrial Revolution speeded that considerably, but it was really the public health revolution, and its spread to the Third World at the end of World War II, that set us galloping. "Before then India was elephants in our mind, and so was Africa—we just had vague notions of these places," said Carl Haub, chief demographer for the Population Reference Bureau. "But then the United Nations started very effective campaigns to raise health standards." Vaccines and antibiotics came all at once, and right behind came population. In Sri Lanka life expectancy was rising two years every twelve months.[12] How much difference did this make? Consider the United States: if people still died at the same age and rate as they did at the turn of the century, America's population would be 140 million, not 270 million.[13]

If it's relatively easy to explain why populations grew so fast after World War II, it's much harder to explain why that growth is now slowing. Experts confidently supply answers, many of them contradictory: "development is the best contraceptive," or education, or the empowerment of women, or hard times that force families to postpone children. For each example, you can find a counterexample. Ninety-seven percent of women in the Arab sheikdom of Oman know about contraception, and yet they have 6.2 children apiece.[14] Turks used contraception at the same rate as the Japanese, but their birthrate was twice as high.[15] And so on. It's not AIDS that will slow population growth, save in a few African countries. It's not horrors like the civil war in Rwanda, which claimed half a million lives, a figure the planet restocks in two days. All that matters is how often individual men and women decide that they want to reproduce. "There is no way to predict fertility change in contemporary societies," says Harvard demographer Nicholas Eberstadt. "Societies of the modern world and the recorded past exhibit a breathtaking diversity of relationships between economic, demographic and social conditions."[16]

Will this drop continue? It better. Right now women in the developing world are averaging four children apiece, down from six; the U.N. projections assume that number will quickly drop to two, the rate at which population growth eventually stabilizes. If fertility levels stall at current levels, population would reach the absurd figure of 296 billion by 2150. Even if it drops to 2.5 kids per woman and then stops falling, the population would still reach an only slightly less absurd 28 billion.[17]

But let's trust that this time the nose-counters have got it right. Let's trust that we're in the home stretch, that we've come around the corner. Let's trust that the planet's population really will double only one more time. Even so, this is a good news–bad news joke. The good news is, we won't grow forever; we won't each of us have to stand on our own small patch of soil, surrounded by a sea of brethren. This has led some to say that we don't need to worry about population. Ben Wattenberg, writing in *The New York Times Magazine* last November, declared, "The population explosion is over."[18]

But the bad news is that there are 6 billion of us already, a number the world strains to support. One more near-doubling—4 or 5 billion more people—will nearly double that strain. Will these be the 5 billion straws that snap the camel's back?

•   •   •

A bear is a bear is a bear, unto the generations. He doesn't wake up one spring and decide he's going to eat six times as many beechnuts as the year before. Humans are more difficult.

We've answered the question "How many of us will there be?" But to figure out how near we are to any limits, we need to ask something else: *How big are we?* Which is not so simple. Not only do we vary vastly one from another in how much food and energy and water and minerals we each consume, but we vary over time. Someone once tried to calculate the amount of energy we used each day. In hunter-gatherer times, it was about 2,500 calories, all of it food we—yes—hunted or gathered. That is the energy equivalent of the daily intake of a common dolphin. Modern human beings use 31,000 calories apiece, most of it in the form of fossil fuel. That's the equivalent of a pilot whale. And the average American uses six times as much as that—as much as a sperm whale.[19] We have become, in other words, different people than we used to be. Not kinder or unkinder, not deeper or more stupid—our natures seem to have changed little since Homer. We've just gotten bigger. We appear to be the same species with the same-sized stomachs, but we aren't; it's as if we're each trailing a big Macy's parade balloon around behind us, feeding it constantly. We are sperm whales cleverly disguised as *Homo sapiens*.

So it doesn't do much good to stare idly out the window of your 737 as you fly from New York to Los Angeles and note that there's *plenty* of empty space down there. Sure enough, you could crowd lots more people into the nation or the planet. The entire world population could fit into Texas and each person could have an area equal to the floor space of a typical U.S. home.[20] Hell, if people were willing to stand, everyone on earth could fit comfortably into half of Rhode Island.[21] Holland is crowded and it's doing just fine.

But this ignores the balloons above our heads, our hungry shadow selves, our sperm whale appetites. As soon as we started farming, we started setting aside extra land to support ourselves. Now each of us needs not only our own little plot of cropland and our own little pasture for the meat we eat, but our own little forest for our timber and paper, our own little mine, our own little oil well. Giants have big feet. Some Vancouver scientists tried to calculate this "footprint," and found that while 1.7 million people lived in the 400,000 hectares surrounding their city, they required 8.7 million hectares of land to support them: wheat fields in Alberta, cornfields in Juarez, oilfields in Arabia, cattle fields in Ecuador, tomato fields in California.[22] People exist in Manhattan the same way people exist on the *Mir* space station.

That balloon above our heads can shrink or grow, depending on how we choose to live. Last fall I visited a friend of mine, David Kline, an Amish farmer and writer in rural Ohio. The corn harvest was underway, and we spent the morning cutting stalks and loading them on a horse-drawn wagon for the trip to the silo; we spent the noon hour eating a communal lunch with the other men, a lunch slaughtered and harvested and milked within a few hundred yards of the room we sat in. I spent the heat of the afternoon lying on my back under a big old tree, listening to the cattle lowing in the barn and the clop of hooves on the road. My friend David Kline was not big, in the sense I've been using big; he could have a dozen children and as long as they stayed near the farm, their impact on the world would be fairly small. (And of course, the Amish do have many children—at the small school I visited, they were sitting two to a desk.)

At the moment, though, the *prevailing* wind blows from the other direction, and at gale force. Around the earth, people who once were tiny are, understandably, suddenly growing like Alice when she ate cake. In China in the last decade, per capita income has doubled. Though to us still Lilliputian, people there are twice their old size. They eat much higher on the food chain than they used to—China slaughters more pigs than any nation on earth—and of course a pig takes four pounds of corn to produce one pound of pork.[23] When the United Nations examined sustainable development, it issued a report saying the world's economy needs to grow five to ten times larger to move poor people to an acceptable standard of living. That we needed to become, in essence, five or ten times larger, with all that means for our demands on oil wells and forests.

That sounds almost impossible. For the moment, though, let's not pass judgment, not say we'd be better living like the Amish. We're still just doing math. There are going to be lots of us. We're going to be big. But lots of us in relation to what? Big in relation to what? It could be that compared to the world we inhabit we're still scarce and small. Or not. So now we need to consider a third question: *how big is the earth?*

•   •

Any state wildlife department can tell you how many deer a given area can support, how much browse there is for the deer to eat before they begin to suppress the reproduction of trees, before they begin to starve in the winter. That's how game wardens decide the number of hunting licenses to issue. They can calculate how many wolves a given area can support, too, mostly by counting the number of deer. And so on, up and down the food chain. It's not an exact science, but it's pretty close, at least compared to figuring out the carrying capacity of the earth for human beings, which is an art so dark anyone with any sense stays away from it.

Consider the simplest difficulties. Human beings, unlike deer, can eat almost anything and live at almost any level they choose: hunter-gatherers use 2,500 calories of energy a day, while modern Americans use seventy-five times as much. Human beings, unlike deer, can import what they need from thousands of miles away. And human beings, unlike deer, can figure out new ways to do old things. If *we* needed to browse on hemlock trees to survive, we could crossbreed lush new strains, chop down competing trees, irrigate forests, spray a thousand chemicals, freeze or dry the tender buds at the peak of harvest, genetically engineer new strains—and advertise the merits of pine branches till everyone was ready to switch. The variables are so enormous that professional demographers barely bother even trying to figure out carrying capacity: demographer Joel Cohen reports that at a recent meeting of the Population Association of America exactly none of the more than two hundred symposia dealt with the topic.

But none of that difficulty has stopped other thinkers; this is, after all, as big a question as the world offers. Plato, Euripides, and Polybius are all on record as worrying that we'd run out of food if the population kept growing;[24] for centuries a steady stream of economists, environmentalists, and other forms of zealot and crank have made it their business to issue estimates either dire or benign. The most famous, of course, came from the Reverend Thomas Malthus. Writing in 1798, he proposed that the growth of population, being "geometric," would soon outstrip the supply of food. Though he soon changed his mind and rewrote his famous essay, it's the original version that people have remembered—and lambasted— ever since.[25] Few writers have found critics in as many corners. Not only have conservatives made his name a byword for ludicrous alarmism, but Marx called his essay "a libel on the human race,"[26] Engels believed "we are forever secure from the fear of overpopulation,"[27] and even Mao attacked him by name, saying that "of all things in the world people are the most precious."[28]

Each new generation of Malthusians have made new predictions that the end was near, and they have been proven conclusively wrong. Sometimes they richly deserved their fate: William Vogt, writing in his 1948 book *Road to Survival,* attributed population growth in Asia to "untrammelled copulation" by "the backward billion."[29] Others thought more compassionately. Fairfield Osborn, writing in 1953, mourned that India would starve and the United States would not be able to help feed her. He had watched the Dust Bowl, "when the sun was darkened from the Rocky Mountains to the Atlantic by vast clouds of soil particles borne from the denuded western grasslands," so it was no surprise when his careful calculations of cropland led him to conclude "we have about come to land's end."[30]

The late 1960s saw a new upsurge of Malthusian panic. In 1967, William and Paul Paddock published a book called *Famine—1975!* that contained triage lists for countries:

Egypt: Can't-be-Saved
Tunisia: Should Receive Food
India: Can't-be-Saved[31]

Almost simultaneously, Paul Ehrlich wrote in his best-selling book *The Population Bomb* that "the battle to feed all of humanity is over. In the 1970s, the world will undergo famines—hundreds of millions of people will starve to death."[32] It all seemed so certain, so in keeping with a world soon to be darkened by the first oil crisis.

But that's not how it worked out, of course. India fed herself; the United States still ships surplus grain around the world. As the astute Harvard social scientist Amartya Sen points out, "food is much cheaper to buy today than it was in Malthus's time, and also than during recent decades." So far, in other words, the world has more or less supported us. Plenty of people starve—60 percent of children in South Asia have their growth stunted by malnutrition[33]—but both the total number and the percentage have dropped in recent decades, thanks mainly to the successes of the Green Revolution. Food production has tripled since World War II, outpacing even population growth.[34] We may be giants, but we are clever giants.

So Malthus is wrong. Over and over again he is wrong. No prophet has ever been proved wrong more times. In each generation Malthusians have risen up to say he is about to be proved right, and in each generation they have been left looking silly. At the moment, his stock is especially low: a group of technological optimists has arisen that believe people will continue to increase their standard of living precisely *because* they increase their numbers. Their intellectual fountainhead is a brilliant Danish economist named Ester Boserup, a sort of anti-Malthus, who in 1965 argued that the gloomy reverend had it backward. The more people, said Boserup, the more progress. Take agriculture as an example. The first farmers, she pointed out, were slash-and-burn cultivators, who might farm a plot for a year or two and then move on, not returning for maybe two decades. But as population grew, they had to return more frequently to the same plot. That meant problems: compacted, depleted, weedy soils. But those new problems meant new solutions: hoes, manure, compost, crop rotation, irrigation.[35] Even in this century, she said, "demand-induced invention" meant that "intensive systems of agriculture replaced extensive systems," accelerating the rate of growth of food production.[36]

Her closely argued examples have given rise to a less cautious group of popularizers, who point out that standards of living have risen the world over even as population has grown. "The most important benefit that population growth confers on an economy is an increase in the stock of useful knowledge," writes Julian Simon, the best known of these so-called cornucopians, who died earlier this year.[37] You might run out of copper, but who cares? The mere fact of shortage will lead someone to invent a substitute. "The main fuel to speed our progress is our stock of knowledge, and the brake is our lack of imagination. The ultimate resource is people— skilled, spirited, and hopeful people who will exert their wills and imaginations for their own benefit, and so, inevitably, for the benefit of us all."[38]

Julian Simon drives environmentalists crazy. He advised President Reagan; he shows up on the cover of magazine after magazine (*Wired*, the technobible, called him "The Doomslayer");[39] he even has his own acolytes to spread the gospel. (Ben Wattenberg, for instance, an aggressively cheerful syndicated columnist who celebrates *everything* about the modern age: "Once-useless rocks became known as 'coal,' once-useless fluids became known as 'oil,' other once-useless rocks became known as 'uranium,' and all soon became known as 'fuel.' Using human intellect, that fuel can be used to make an electric toothbrush go jiggle-jiggle when you press a button.")[40] But Simon and his ilk owe their success to this: they have been right. The world has behaved as they have predicted. India hasn't starved. Food is cheap. We may be giants, but we have giant brains, giant enough that we've unlocked many of the earth's secrets. Malthus has once more been proved wrong.

But Malthus never goes away. The idea that we might grow too big can only be disproved for the moment, never for good. We might always be on the threshold of a special time, when the mechanisms described by Boserup and Simon stop working. It is true that Malthus was wrong when the population doubled from 750 million to 1.5 billion. It is true that Malthus was wrong when the population doubled from 1.5 billion to 3 billion. It is true that Malthus was wrong when the population doubled from 3 billion to 6 billion. But it's also true that a car can go 15 miles an hour safely, and 30, and 60, and maybe even 120 on a nice straight highway. Even at Indy, though, they haven't gotten up to 240. Will Malthus still be wrong fifty years from now?

•　　•　　•

If you wanted to make the case that the next doubling, the one we're now experiencing, might be the difficult one, you could as easily begin with Peter Vitousek as anyone else. In 1986 the Stanford biologist decided to calculate how much of the earth's "primary productivity" went to support humans. He added together the grain we ate ourselves, the corn we fed our cows, and the forests we cut for timber and paper; he added in the losses in food as we overgrazed grassland and turned it into desert. And when he was done adding, the number he came up with was 40 percent. We used 40 percent of everything the world's plants don't need to keep themselves alive; directly or indirectly we eat 40 percent of what's possible to eat. "That's a relatively large number," says Vitousek. "It should give pause to people who think we are far from any limits." Though he never drops the measured tone of an academic, Vitousek speaks with considerable emphasis: "There's a sense among economists that we're *so* far from any biophysical limits. I think that's not supported by the evidence."[41]

And if you want an antidote to the good cheer of someone like Julian Simon, sit down with a scientist like Cornell biologist David Pimentel. He's a true believer, too, but he believes we're in big trouble. Odd facts stud his conversation. Did you know a nice head of iceberg lettuce is 95 percent water, just 50 calories of energy, but that it takes 400 calories of energy to grow it in California's Central Valley, and another 1,800 to ship it east? ("There's practically no nutrition in the damn stuff anyway. Cabbage is a lot better, and we can grow it here.")[42] Pimentel has devoted the last three decades to tracking the planet's capacity, and he believes we're already too crowded, that the earth can only support 2 billion people over the long run at a middle-class standard of living, and that trying to support more is doing great damage. He's spent considerable time studying soil erosion, for instance. Every time a raindrop hits exposed ground, it's like a small explosion, launching soil particles into the air. If it's on a slope, more than half of the soil contained in those splashes is carried downhill.[43] If you leave the crop residue—the cornstalks, say—in the field after harvest, that helps shield the soil. The raindrop doesn't hit as hard. But in the developing world, where fire-wood is now scarce, peasants burn those cornstalks for cooking fuel. About 60 percent of crop residues in China and 90 percent in Bangladesh are removed and burned, he says. When planting season comes, dry soils simply blow away. "Our measuring stations pick up Chinese soil in the Hawaiian air when plowing time comes. Every year in Florida we pick up African soils in the wind when they start to plow."[44]

The very things that made the Green Revolution so stunning—that allowed the last doubling to be relatively pain-less—now cause trouble. Irrigation, for instance, waters 17 percent of all arable land and helps produce a third of all crops. But flooded soils are baked by the sun, the water evaporates, and the minerals in the irrigation water are deposited on the land. A typical hectare will accumulate two to five tons of salt annually, and eventually plants won't grow. Maybe 10 percent of all irrigated land is affected.[45]

Or think about fresh water for human use. Plenty of rain falls on the earth's surface, but most of it evaporates or roars down to the ocean in spring floods. We're left with about 9,000 cubic kilometers of potential fresh water, which would still be enough, except that it's not very well distributed around the globe. And we're not exactly conservationists—we use seven times as much water as we used in 1900. Already 20 percent of the world lacks access to potable water[46] and fights over water roil many regions; already the Colorado River dries out in the desert long before it reaches the Sea of Cortés, making what mid-century conservationist Aldo Leopold called "a milk and honey wilderness" into "the most inhospitable terrain on the North American continent";[47] already the Yellow River runs dry a third of the year; already only 2 percent of the Nile's flow makes it to the ocean.[48] And we need more water all the time. Producing a ton of grain consumes a thousand tons of water—that's how much the wheat plant breathes out as it grows.[49] "We estimated that biotechnology might cut the amount of water a plant uses by 10 percent," says Pimentel. "But the biologists tell us that's optimistic—they remind us that water's a pretty important part of photosynthesis. Maybe we can get 5 percent."[50]

What these scientists are saying is simple: human ingenuity can turn sand into silicon chips, allowing the creation of millions of utterly fascinating home pages on the utterly fascinating World Wide Web, but that human ingenuity cannot forever turn dry sand into soil that will grow food: www.twinkies.com, but not www.wheat.more. And there are signs that these skeptics are right—that we are approaching certain physical limits.

I said earlier that food production had grown even faster than population since the Second World War. Year after year the yield of wheat and corn and rice rocketed up about 3 percent annually. It's a favorite statistic of the eternal optimists. Julian Simon, in his 1981 book *The Ultimate Resource*, has a chart showing just how fast this growth was, and how it continually cut the cost of food. "The obvious implication of this historical trend toward cheaper food—a trend that probably extends back to the beginning of agriculture—is that real prices for food will continue to drop. . . . It is a fact that portends more drops in price and even less scarcity in the future."[51]

A year or two after Simon's book was published, however, the data began to curve in a new direction. That rocketing upward growth in grain production ceased; now the gains were coming in tiny increments, too small to keep pace with the growth of the population. The world reaped its largest harvest of grain per capita in 1984; since then, the amount of corn and wheat and rice per person has fallen 6 percent. Grain stockpiles have shrunk to less than two months' supply.[52]

No one knows quite why. The collapse of the Soviet Union contributed to the trend; cooperative farms suddenly found their fertilizer supply shut off, and spare parts for the tractor hard to come by. But there were other causes, too, all around the world: the salinization of irrigated fields, the erosion of topsoil, the conversion of prime farmland into homes, and all the other things environmentalists had been warning about for years. It's possible we'll still turn it around, start grain production rocketing upward again. Charles Mann, writing in *Science*, quotes experts who believe a "gigantic, multi-year, multi-billion-dollar scientific effort, a kind of agricultural 'person-on-the-moon project,'" might do the trick. The next great hope of the optimists is genetic engineering, and indeed scientists have managed to induce pesticide and herbicide resistance in some plants. To get more yield, though, you've got to get a cornstalk to put out another ear, and conventional breeding may have already taken that nearly as far as you can go and still have a viable plant. You need roots and stems or there's no plant to hold the grain; already these have been pared close to the theoretical minimum. There's a sense we're running into walls.

We won't start producing *less* food. Wheat is not like oil, where the flow from the spigot will simply slow to a trickle one day. But we may be getting to the point where the gains will be small and hard to come by—the spectacular increases may be behind us. Even an optimistic researcher told Mann that "producing higher yields will no longer be like unveiling a new model of car. We won't be pulling off the sheet and there it is, a twofold increase." Instead, the process will be "incremental, tortuous, and slow."[53] And there are 5 billion more of us still to come.

You can find real doomsayers who think we've already gone much too far. Their touchstone is Easter Island, that dot in the Pacific known mostly for its statues of guys with giant heads. No one knew what had become of the civilization that built them; by the time Europeans arrived, they found only a small and impoverished tribe. The island appeared to have only enough good soil to support 3,000 to 4,000 people. There were no trees at all—how could people possibly have built the beams to lever the great stones into place? It was all a bafflement.

The prevailing theory, proposed by classicist John Macmillan Brown, was that Easter Island was just one of many islands in an archipelago, and that it was used as a mausoleum for kings; some geological event, perhaps a volcano, had sunk the other islands, where the workers and the trees had lived, leaving only the riddle of the giant heads above the waves.[54] Fifty years later, though, another explanation emerged. Easter Island, according to this account, was a world unto itself, a solitary island once heavily forested. And for a time, its inhabitants had been very successful, so successful that they had the leisure time to build big stone heads. So successful that they soon overpopulated the island and began to wreck its ecosystems, destroying them so completely that when they were done only a miserable relict remained to puzzle the archaeologists.

The point of this autopsy, according to author William Catton, is simple: islands can *temporarily* provide for lots of people, but only at the cost of damaging their ecosystems, and so reducing dramatically their long-term capacity.[55] "Overshoot" was the term he coined, and in a book of the same name he said it applied not only to islands but also to planets. Ours in particular. Malthus did make a mistake, says Catton, but not the one he's usually charged with. Instead, he didn't understand that for *a little while* people could exceed the earth's carrying capacity. But eventually it would catch up with them. "Nature is going to require reduction of human dominance over the world ecosystem,"[56] he writes, a grim exercise that may leave us so degraded that someday we fight with each other for scraps of food.[57]

It's hard for any of us to accept Catton's conclusions, and not just because they're unspeakably depressing. It's hard because so far they haven't come true—they run counter to our experience. So far, we're still fed; gas is cheap at the pump; the supermarket grows an acre larger every few years. For three decades we've been warned about approaching limits and we've never quite gotten to them. So maybe—and how tempting to believe!—they don't really exist. For every Catton, a Julian Simon; for every Paul Ehrlich, a man like former World Bank chief economist Lawrence Summers, who says: "There are no limits to the carrying capacity of the Earth that are likely to bind at any time in the foreseeable future."[58] And we are talking about the future—there's nothing you can *prove*.

But you can calculate *risks*, figure the *odds* that each side might be right. The demographer Joel Cohen made the most thorough attempt to do so in his 1995 book that bore the straightforward title *How Many People Can the Earth Support?* Cohen collected and examined every estimate of carrying capacity made in recent decades, from a Harvard oceanographer who thought in 1970 we might have food enough for 40 billion people to a Brown University researcher who calculated a few years later that we might be able to sustain 5.9 billion (our present population), but only if we were all vegetarians. One study demonstrated that if photosynthesis were the limiting factor we might squeeze a trillion people on the planet; meanwhile, an Australian economist proved that the earth could support a population of 28 billion, then a decade later recalibrated the figure and concluded it was more like 157 billion. None of the individual studies is wise enough to examine every variable, to reach by itself the "right" number. When Cohen averages out all the dozens of studies, however, he uncovers something pretty interesting: the median low value for the planet's carrying capacity is 7.7 billion people, and the median high value is 12 billion. That, of course, is precisely the range the United Nations predicts we will reach by the middle of the next century. In other words:

> The human population of the Earth now travels in the zone where a substantial fraction of scholars have estimated upper limits on human population size.... The possibility must be considered that the Earth has reached, or will reach within half a century, the maximum number the Earth can support in modes of life that we and our children and their children will choose to want.[59]

As an example, let's consider one of our classic symbols of abundance. What do you tell your kid sister when she breaks up with her boyfriend? "There's lots of fish in the ocean." But we may need a new metaphor, because if you want a sense of what it feels like to be somewhere near a limit, somewhere on the far edge of abundance, then you need to consider fish.

After increasing twenty-five-fold since 1900, the fish catch from the world's oceans peaked in 1989 at nearly 90 million tons, and then began to drop. Partly, that's because fishermen have behaved like human beings, which is to say shortsightedly: bigger and bigger boats with better and better electronics have hunted down more and more fish. In the Dutch region of the North Sea, for instance, every single square foot of the sea bottom is dragged by a trawler at least once a year. In Indonesia, "fishermen" routinely kill off miles of coral reef with blasts of cyanide in order to collect the poison-stunned fish for sale to fancy restaurants. Around the world huge nets bring in millions of tons of "by-catch" each year—"trash fish" that are tossed back overboard, usually to die because their swim bladders burst during the quick ascent in the net. Meanwhile, the most expensive fish call forth every technological marvel. Spotter airplanes circle the North Atlantic, radioing boats as soon as they spot bluefin tuna, one 750-pound specimen of which sold for $83,500 on the Tokyo market. When the Japanese squid fleet turns on their high-powered lights at night to lure the creatures, you can see the flash from space. Carl Safina, in his book *Song for the Blue Ocean,* put it this way: "The last buffalo hunt is occurring on the rolling blue prairies of the ocean."[60]

But even that kind of frenzy—which could, theoretically, be fixed with law and common sense—only explains part of the story. To really understand the limits to abundance you need to go to places where people *have* been careful, like the great salmon fishery in Alaska's Bristol Bay. From there, follow the Ugashik River up to its source at Ugashik Lake, where each summer a crew of college boys mans the fish-counting ladders. Every hour one of them climbs a rickety scaffolding next to the river, sits down on a plank, and stares into the water. As he sees the flash of a salmon swimming upstream in the clear water to spawn, he clicks the clicker in his hand like the ticket-taker at a high school dance. And then after a few minutes he climbs down, returns to the shack, and radios the numbers in to Jeff Regnart, the state fisheries biologist a hundred miles away in the town of King Salmon.

Regnart's job is fairly simple: making sure that salmon make it upstream past the fishermen in sufficient numbers to spawn, and to guarantee that there will be a good run when this class returns on *its* spawning run four years hence. You don't need all the fish, or even most of them, to lay or fertilize eggs. In a good year, 10 million fish might return to the Ugashik, of which 700,000 will lay enough eggs for a successful spawn; once they've made it upstream, the fishermen in the boats down by the ocean can take the rest. But if those 700,000 don't appear, then there's no fishing. Each afternoon last July, which was a slow sockeye season, Regnart went on the radio to relay the grim news to the fishermen. "Our commitment is to get the escapement above all," he says. "There's no compromise in the middle of the year to say we're going to trim it this year to let you guys cover your expenses. Our job is to hold that line, however much we're getting beat up." And so the fish always come back.

But they don't—and this is the point—come back in ever-greater numbers. They don't multiply simply because our population multiplies. Over the decades, the number of fish returning to Bristol Bay has fluctuated, but within a fairly tight range. It is as big as it's going to get. "These are natural systems," says Regnart. "You can't just go and add fertilizer to the lakes to grow more fish. These systems are much too large to manipulate that way—if we tried, we'd screw up."[61]

We are, in other words, maxed out. We're taking all the fish from the sea that there are to take. You can, of course, grow more fish by farming them in ponds. And increasingly that's what we're doing; it's the "clever" way out of this fix. But farming fish, sadly, is not like netting them from the ocean. Once they're in a pond or a cage you have to feed them. "The nice thing about the oceans," says Lester Brown, the director of the Worldwatch Institute, "was that what you had to buy was diesel fuels or sails. But when you start a fish farm, you've created a wet feedlot."

Many fish—salmon, for instance—are carnivores, high-on-the-food-chain foragers. If you want to raise them in a pond, you need to dump in fish meal for them to eat. Increasingly, the ocean fishermen who have decimated stocks of fish like cod and haddock catch bony little pilchards and anchovies instead, mostly for use as salmon chow. Instead of fish catching their dinner, that is, we catch it for them. Other species, like catfish, thrive on a nice diet of cornmeal; a catfish farm is exactly like a chicken farm, except that the chickens swim. "It takes about 2.2 pounds of grain to grow a broiler to market size," says Lester Brown. "In a catfish farm it takes about two pounds."[62]

And here, of course, we're right back to our question of limits. Cornmeal is getting scarce. As we saw already, there's less grain per person than there used to be. We need 2 million more tons of protein each year just to supply the growth in population, and since oceanic fish catches are no longer increasing, that protein has to come from land. If it's going to come from a fish farm, that means 4 million more tons of grain.

The math is no fun to do, not for fish or for anything else. Because we live in a special time.

chapter

four

THROUGHOUT THE 10,000 YEARS THAT COMPRISE HUMAN HIS-
TORY, THE PLANET—THE PHYSICAL PLANET—HAS BEEN A STABLE
place. In every single year of those 10,000, there have been
earthquakes, volcanoes, hurricanes, cyclones, typhoons,
floods, forest fires, sandstorms, hailstorms, plagues, crop fail-
ures, heat waves, cold spells, blizzards, and droughts. But they
have never shaken the basic physical stability of the planet as
a whole. Its climate has usually changed slowly, so that people
from one generation to the next would never notice; some of
its land areas—the Mediterranean region, for instance—have
been deforested never to recover, but these shifts so far have
always been local.

Among other things, this stability has made possible the
insurance industry, has underwritten the underwriters. Insur-
ers can analyze the risk in any venture because they know the
basic ground rules. If you want to build a house on the coast of

Florida, they can calculate with reasonable certainty the chance that it will be hit by a hurricane and the speed of the winds circling that hurricane's eye. If they couldn't do that, then they'd have no way to set your premium—they'd just be gambling. They're always gambling a little, of course: they don't know if that hurricane is coming next year or next century. But the earth's physical stability is the house edge in this casino. As Julian Simon himself points out, "a prediction based on past data can be sound if it is sensible to assume that the past and future belong to the same statistical universe."[1]

So what does it mean that, alone among the earth's great pools of money and power, the earth's insurance companies are beginning to take the idea of global climate change quite seriously? What does it mean that their payouts for weather-related damage climbed from $16 billion during the 1980s to $48 billion so far in the 1990s?[2] What does it mean that many of the top European insurance executives have begun consulting constantly with Greenpeace about issues like global warming? What does it mean that insurance giant Swiss Re, which paid out 400 million Swiss francs in the wake of Hurricane Andrew, ran an ad in the *Financial Times* showing its corporate logo bent sideways by a storm?[3]

It means, I think, that the possibility that we live on a new earth cannot be discounted entirely as the fever-dreams of cranks. In the previous chapter we attempted to calculate carrying capacity for the world as we have always known it, the world we were born into. All of Joel Cohen's estimates, all of Julian Simon's examples, all of Lester Brown's alarums—they concerned the planet we've long known. They concern earth. But what if, all of a sudden, we live on some other planet? On Earth2?

It may seem as if we're wandering far from the topic of population, leaving behind the question of single-child families. In fact, we're getting closer to the nub of things. We're getting warmer.

•   •   •

Born in Vermont, George Perkins Marsh grew up to be a diplomat, a man of wide travels and wide learning. In 1864 he published his masterpiece, *Man and Nature*, which set out to:

> indicate the character and, approximately, the extent of the changes produced by human action in the physical conditions of the globe we inhabit; to point out the dangers of imprudence and the necessity of caution in all operations which, on a large scale, interfere with the spontaneous arrangements of the organic or inorganic world; to suggest the possibility and the importance of the restoration of disturbed harmonies; and, incidentally, to illustrate the doctrine that man is, in both kind and degree, a power of a higher order than any of the other forms of animated life.[4]

It marked, in other words, the first systematic attempt to gauge the relative size of man and everything else. Marsh explained in great detail the phenomena he had seen all around him as a boy—how cutting of forests changed the local climate by leading to great spring floods when the snowmelt poured down the naked hillsides and regular summer droughts as the streams dried up. And his book mattered: my home, the Adirondack Mountains of New York, was preserved as the greatest wilderness of the East in part because downstate business interests read Marsh and feared that continued clear-cutting would silt up the Hudson. He was a prophet, truly. But though he could sense that we were growing larger, men and women were then still small in relation to the earth.

Ninety years later, in 1955, a second and more sweeping assessment took place—Princeton held an international symposium on the topic "Man's Role in the Changing of the Earth." By this time carbon, sulfur, phosphorus, and nitrogen were pouring into the atmosphere, deforestation was already widespread, and world population was nearing 3 billion.[5] Still, by comparison to the present, we remained a puny race. Cars were as yet novelties in most places. The tropical forests were still intact, as were much of the ancient woods of the West Coast, Canada, and Siberia. The world's economy was one-sixth its present size.[6] By most calculations, we've used more natural resources since 1955 than in all of human history to that time.

Which set the stage for yet another symposium, this one organized in 1987 by Clark University in Massachusetts. And this time even the title made it clear what was happening: not "Man and Nature," not "Man's Role in Changing the Face of the Earth," but "The Earth as Transformed by Human Actions." They were no longer talking about local changes or about future predictions. "In our judgment," they said, "the biosphere has accumulated, or is on its way to accumulating, such a magnitude and variety of changes that it may be said to have been transformed."[7]

Some of the changes that they noted were fascinating but not vital. When we cut down trees to create cropland, for instance, we reduce the earth's "roughness" by two-thirds or more; when we turn it into desert, we reduce its roughness another thirty times, increasing local wind speeds, the amount of turbulence, and even the transfer of momentum between the earth's surface and the atmosphere.[8] We've built so many reservoirs in the northern hemisphere that we've altered the planet's center of gravity enough to infinitesimally increase the speed with which it spins.[9]

Beyond such curiosities, there are other, greater changes, and they come from a direction that Malthus didn't consider. He and most of his successors were transfixed by *sources*—by figuring out whether and how we could find enough trees or corn or oil. We're good at finding more stuff, it turns out; as the price rises, we look harder. The lights never did go out, despite many predictions to the contrary on the first Earth Day; we've found more oil, and though it will run out someday, we've got lots and lots of coal. Meanwhile, we're driving big cars again, and gas at the pump costs less than it did on the day the first filling station was built. Who can believe in limits while driving a Suburban? But perhaps, like an audience watching a magician wave his wand, we've been distracted from the real story.

And that real story was told, at its most basic, in the next attempt to calculate our size, a special issue of *Science* magazine published in the summer of 1997. *Science* is, well, a *scientific* magazine (one of the other articles in this special issue was titled "Chlorine 36 in Fossil Rat Urine: An Archive of Cosmogenic Nuclide Deposition"). But the editors, including Jane Lubchenco, president of the American Association for the Advancement of Science, spoke quite clearly in the main article. Forget man "transforming" nature; we live, they concluded, on "a human-*dominated* planet," where "no ecosystem on Earth's surface is free of pervasive human influence."[10] It's not that we're running out of stuff; what we're running out of are what the scientists call "sinks." Places to put the *by-products* of our large appetites. Not garbage dumps—we could go on using Pampers till the end of time and still have empty space left to toss them away. But the atmospheric equivalent of garbage dumps.

We pretty quickly figured out that there were limits on how much coal smoke we could pour into the air of a single city. It took a while longer to figure out that building ever-higher smokestacks merely lofted their haze farther afield, raining down acid on whatever mountain range lay to the east. Even that, however, we are slowly fixing with scrubbers and different mixes of fuel. What we can't repair so easily, though, are the new kinds of pollution. They don't come from something going wrong—some engine without a catalytic converter, some wastewater pipe without a filter, some smokestack without a scrubber. They come instead from things going as they're supposed to go, simply at such a high volume that they overwhelm the planet. They come from normal human life, but there are so many of us living those normal lives that something abnormal is happening. And that something is so different from the old forms of pollution that it confuses the issue even to use the word.

Consider nitrogen, for instance. Almost 80 percent of the atmosphere is nitrogen gas. But before plants can absorb it directly from the air, it must become "fixed," bonded with hydrogen or oxygen. Nature does this trick with certain kinds of algae and soil bacteria, and with lightning. Before human beings began to alter the nitrogen cycle, these mechanisms provided 90 to 150 million tons of nitrogen a year. Now human activity adds 130 to 150 million more tons. It's not pollution—it's essential. Vaclav Smil, writing in *Scientific American*, says "nitrogen-rich fertilizer has effectively done away with what for ages had been a fundamental restriction on food production. Human society has one key chemical industry to thank for the abundance [of food]—the producers of nitrogen fertilizer." At least "two billion people are alive because the proteins in their bodies are built with nitrogen" that came from synthetic fertilizers—it has helped underwrite our population growth.[11] And we are using more of it all the time—half the industrial nitrogen fertilizer used in human history has been applied since 1984. As a result, coastal waters and estuaries bloom with toxic algae and dwindle in oxygen concentrations, killing fish; as a result, nitrous oxide destroys stratospheric ozone and traps solar radiation. And once it's in the air, it stays there for hundreds of years.[12]

Or consider methane. It's not pollution, exactly, either—it's what comes out the back of a cow or the top of a termite mound or out from the bottom of a rice paddy. But thanks to our determination to grow more rice, raise more cattle, and cut down more tropical forest (which causes termite populations to explode), methane concentrations in the atmosphere are two-and-a-half times higher than they've been in the past 160,000 years. And methane traps heat, traps it very efficiently.[13]

Or consider carbon dioxide. In fact, concentrate on carbon dioxide. If you had to pick one problem to obsess about in the next fifty years, you'd do well to make it CO_2, which is not pollution either. Carbon *mon*oxide is pollution—it kills you if you breathe enough of it. But carbon *di*oxide, carbon with two oxygen atoms, can't do a blessed thing to you. If you're reading this indoors, you're breathing more CO_2 than you'll ever get outside. For generations, in fact, engineers said an engine burned clean if it produced only water vapor and carbon dioxide.

But here's the first catch: that engine produces a *lot* of CO_2. A gallon of gas weighs eight pounds. If you burn it in your car, five and a half pounds of carbon in the form of carbon dioxide comes spewing out the back. It doesn't matter if you drive a 1958 Chevy or a 1998 Saab. And there's no filter that can reduce that flow—it's an inevitable by-product of fossil fuel combustion. Which is why it's been piling up in the atmosphere ever since the Industrial Revolution. Before we started burning oil and coal and gas, the atmosphere contained about 280 parts per million CO_2. Now it contains about 360. Unless we do everything we can think of to eliminate fossil fuel from our diet, the air will test out at 560 parts per million fifty or sixty years from now, whether you sample it in the South Bronx or at the South Pole.

And here's the second catch: as we all know by now this clean, natural, common element that we are now adding to every cubic foot of atmosphere that surrounds us has one interesting property. Its molecular structure traps heat that would otherwise radiate back out to space. Far more even than methane and nitrous oxide, it drives global warming, the greenhouse effect, climate change. Far more than any other single phenomenon, it is turning the earth we were born on into a new planet.

Remember, this is not pollution as we have known it. In the spring of 1997, the EPA issued its Ten-Year Air Quality and Emissions Trends report. Carbon monoxide was down 37 percent since 1986, lead was down 78 percent, particulates had dropped by nearly a quarter.[14] If you lived in the San Fernando Valley, you saw the mountains more often than you did a decade before. The air was *cleaner*, but it was also *different*, richer with CO_2. And its new composition may change almost everything.

Ten years ago I wrote a book called *The End of Nature*, which was the first volume for a general audience about carbon dioxide and climate change, an early attempt to show that we now dominated this earth. Even then, less than a decade ago, global warming was only a hypothesis—a strong hypothesis, one gaining credibility all the time, but a hypothesis nonetheless. By the late 1990s, though, it had become a fact. For ten years, with heavy funding from governments around the world, scientists launched satellites, monitored weather balloons, studied clouds. Their work culminated in the fall of 1995 when the U.N.'s Intergovernmental Panel on Climate Change released its long-awaited report. The panel's 1,500 scientists from every corner of the globe summed up their findings in this dry but historic bit of understatement: "The balance of evidence suggests that there is a discernible human influence on global climate."[15] That is to say, we are heating up the planet, heating it substantially. If we don't reduce emissions of carbon dioxide and other gases, the panel warned, temperatures will probably rise 3.6 degrees Fahrenheit by 2100, and perhaps as much as 6.3 degrees.

You may think you've already heard a lot about global warming. But most of our sense of the problem is well behind the curve. Here's the current news: the changes are already well underway. Though politicians and businessmen still talk about "future risks," their rhetoric is outdated. This is not a problem for the distant future, or even the near future. The planet has already heated a degree or more, heated faster than at any time in human history. We're a quarter of the way into the greenhouse era and the results are already appearing. From a new heaven filled with nitrogen, methane, and carbon, a new earth is being born. If some alien astronomer is watching us, she's doubtless puzzled. It's the most obvious effect of our numbers, our appetites, and the key to understanding why the size of our populations suddenly poses such a risk.

What does this new world feel like? For one thing, it's stormier than it was before. A 1997 study by Thomas Karl of the National Oceanic and Atmospheric Administration showed that total winter precipitation had increased 10 percent and that "extreme precipitation events"—blizzards and rainstorms that dumped more than two inches of precipitation in twenty-four hours—had jumped 20 percent in the United States since 1900. That's because warmer air holds more water vapor than the colder atmosphere of the old earth; more water evaporates from the ocean, meaning more clouds, more rain, more snow. Engineers designing storm sewers, bridges, and culverts used to plan for what they called the "hundred-year storm." That is, they built to withstand the worst flooding or wind that history led them to expect in the course of a century. Since that history no longer applies, "there really isn't a hundred-year event anymore," according to Karl.[16] "We seem to be getting these storms-of-the-century every couple of years."[17] When Grand Forks disappeared beneath the Red River in the spring of 1997, some meteorologists referred to it as "a 500-year flood." Meaning, essentially, that all bets are off. Meaning that these aren't acts of God. "If you look out your window, part of what you see in terms of weather is produced by ourselves," says Karl. "If you look out the window fifty years from now, we're going to be responsible for more of it."[18]

Twenty percent more bad storms; 10 percent more snow. These are enormous numbers; it's like opening the newspaper to read that the average American is suddenly seven feet tall. And the same study found increases in drought, too. With more water in the atmosphere, there's less in the soil, according to Kevin Trenberth of the National Center for Atmospheric Research. Those parts of the continent that are normally dry— the eastern side of the mountains, the plains and deserts—are even drier, as the higher average temperatures evaporate more of what rain does fall. "You get wilting plants and eventually drought faster than you would otherwise," says Trenberth. And when the rain does come, it's apt to be so heavy that much of it runs off before it can sink into the ground.[19]

So—wetter, drier. And just *different*.

Since 1958, Charles Keeling of the Scripps Institution of Oceanography in California has run the world's single most crucial scientific instrument from a small hut halfway up the side of Hawaii's Mauna Loa volcano. It's a creaking old thing—when I visited, the technicians were hunting for a new source of vacuum tubes—but it continues without fail to track the amount of carbon dioxide in the atmosphere. The graph paper that spools endlessly out of the printer by its side shows that this most important greenhouse gas has steadily increased for forty years. That's the main news.

But it has also shown something else of interest in recent years, a sign that this new atmosphere is changing the planet. Every year the CO_2 levels dip in the spring when plants across the northern hemisphere begin to grow, soaking up carbon dioxide. And every year in the fall decaying plants and soils release CO_2 back into the atmosphere. So along with the steady upward trend, there's an annual seesaw—an oscillation that is suddenly growing more pronounced. The size of that yearly "tooth" on the saw is 20 percent greater than it was in 1964.[20] In other words, according to Keeling's data, the earth is breathing deeper.[21] More vegetation must be growing, stimulated by higher temperatures. And the earth is breathing earlier, too—spring is starting about a week earlier in the 1990s than in the 1960s, said Keeling.[22]

Other scientists had a hard time crediting Keeling's study, the effect seemed so massive. But six months later a team at Boston University reached precisely the same conclusion with a completely different technique. These researchers used satellites to measure the color of sunlight reflected off the ground—when it bounces off green leaves, the light has a different color than when it reflects off bare ground.[23] Their data was even more alarming, because it showed the increase happening with almost lightning speed: by 1991, spring was coming eight days earlier than it had just a decade before above the 45th parallel, a line that runs roughly from Yellowstone to Minneapolis to Boston to Milan to Belgrade to Vladivostok.[24] And that was despite increased snowfall from the wetter atmosphere; the snow was simply melting earlier.[25] The earlier spring led to increased plant growth, which sounds like a benefit—this, after all, is the North American and Russian wheat belt. But as Dr. Cynthia Rosenzweig of NASA's Goddard Institute for Space Studies told the *New York Times*, any such gains may be illusory. For one thing, the satellites were measuring biomass, not yields—tall and leafy plants often produce less grain. Other scientists, the *Times* reported, "say more rapid plant growth can make for less nutritious crops if there are not enough nutrients available in the soil."[26] And it's not clear they'll have the water they need to grow as climate warms; in 1988, the warmest summer yet across the grain belt, harvests plummeted[27] because that same heat that yields more storms also causes extra evaporation. What *is* clear is this: fundamental shifts are underway in the basic operation of the planet. And we are very early yet in the greenhouse era, through perhaps a quarter of the warming that the scientists are predicting.

The changes are so *basic*. The freezing level in the atmosphere—the height where the air temperature reaches 32 degrees Fahrenheit—has been gaining altitude since 1970 at a rate of fifteen feet a year. That is, you have to climb four hundred feet higher up a mountain than you used to before you reach the icy zone. Not surprisingly, tropical and subtropical glaciers are melting at what a team of Ohio State researchers termed "striking" rates.[28] Speaking at a National Press Club roundtable, Ellen Mosley-Thompson, the leader of the Ohio State team, was asked by a reporter if she was sure about her results:

> I don't know quite what to say. I've presented the evidence. I gave you the example of the Quelccaya ice cap. It just comes back to the compilation of what's happening at high elevations: the Lewis glacier on Mt. Kenya has lost forty percent of its mass, in the Ruwenzori range all the glaciers there are in a massive retreat. Everything virtually in Patagonia except for just a few glaciers are retreating. We've seen from Dr. Grabherr's data that plants are moving up the mountains. I frankly don't know what additional evidence you need.[29]

As the glaciers retreat, a key source of fresh water in many tropical countries disappears. These areas are "already water-stressed," Mosley-Thompson told the American Association of Geographers;[30] now they may really be desperate.

As with the tropics, so with the poles—more so, in fact, since every computer model shows the Arctic and the Antarctic warming much faster than the equator as carbon dioxide builds up. University of Kansas scientists manning a research station at Toolik Lake, Alaska, 170 miles north of the Arctic Circle, "have watched the average summer temperatures warm up by about seven degrees" in the last two decades. "Those who remember wearing down-lined summer parkas in the 1970s—before the term 'global warming' existed—have peeled down to T-shirts in recent summers."[31] It rained briefly at the American base on Antarctica's McMurdo Sound during the southern summer of 1997;[32] that's as strange as if it had snowed in Saudi Arabia. None of this necessarily means that the ice caps will soon slide into the sea, turning Tennessee into beachfront; it simply demonstrates radical instability in places that have been stable for many thousands of years. One researcher watched as emperor penguins tried to cope with the early breakup of ice—their young had to jump into the water two weeks ahead of schedule, "probably dooming the juveniles to an early death."[33] They had evolved (like us) on the old earth.

You don't have to go to exotic places to watch the process. Migrating red-winged blackbirds now arrive three weeks earlier in Michigan than they did in 1960.[34] In the Pacific Northwest a symposium of scientists reported in 1996 that the region was warming at four times the world rate. "That the Northwest is warming up fast is not a theory. It's a known fact, based on simple temperature readings," said Richard Gammon, a University of Washington oceanographer.[35]

And you can find the effects of that warming in the largest phenomena. The level of the oceans that cover most of the planet's surface is clearly rising, both because of melting glaciers and because warm water takes up more space than cold; as a result, low-lying Pacific islands already report surges of water washing across the atolls. "It's nice weather and all of a sudden water is pouring into your living room," says one Marshall Islands official. "It's very clear that something is happening in the Pacific and these islands are feeling it."[36] Global warming will be like a much more powerful version of El

Niño, one that covers the entire globe and lasts forever, or at least until the next big asteroid strikes.

If you want to scare yourself with guesses about what might happen in the near future, there's no shortage of possibilities. Scientists have already noted large-scale shifts in the duration of the El Niño ocean warming, a millennia-old phenomenon that influences weather across the hemisphere.[37] In the Arctic the tundra has warmed so much that in some places it now gives off carbon dioxide instead of absorbing it, a switch that could become a potent feedback loop making warming ever worse.[38] And researchers studying glacial cores from the Greenland Ice Sheet recently concluded that climate shifts have happened with incredible rapidity in the past—eighteen degrees in three years during one stretch[39]—which other scientists worry might be enough to flood the oceans with fresh water and change or shut off currents like the Gulf Stream and the North Atlantic that keep Europe far warmer than it would otherwise be.[40] In the words of Columbia University's Wallace Broecker, one of the pioneers of the field, "climate is an angry beast and we are poking it with sticks."[41]

But you don't need worst-case scenarios. Best-case scenarios make the point. The population of the earth is going to nearly double one more time. That will bring it to a level that even the old reliable earth we were born on would be hard-pressed to support. Just at the moment when we need everything to be working as smoothly as possible, we find ourselves inhabiting a new planet, one for which we can make no conceivable estimates of carrying capacity. We have no idea how much wheat this world can grow. We don't know what its politics will be like—not if there are going to be heat waves like the one that killed 733 Chicagoans in a single week,[42] not if 80 million more people are contracting malaria because of warmer weather each year,[43] not if rising sea levels and other effects of climate change create additional tens of millions of environmental refugees,[44] not if a 1.5-degree-Fahrenheit jump in India's temperature could reduce the country's wheat crop by 10 percent or divert its monsoons.[45]

"We appear to be entering a period in which all food-producing systems must function well almost all the time," said one group of experts.[46] But already analyses of corn and other crops show growing variability of yields, as hot weather some summers drives down harvests.[47] Harvard's James McCarthy, who supervised the work of climate scientists from sixty nations for the U.N., put it this way: "If the last 150 years had been marked by the kind of climate instability we are now seeing, the world would never have been able to support its *present* population."[48]

The argument put forth by men like Julian Simon—the argument that human intelligence will get us out of any scrape, the argument that humans are "the ultimate resource," the argument that Malthusian models "simply do not comprehend key elements of people"[49]—all those eloquent and until-now correct arguments rest on the same premise. They presume that human beings mainly change the world for the better. The more the merrier. If we live at a special time, the single most special thing about it may be that we are now apparently degrading the most basic functions of the planet.

It's not that we've never altered our surroundings before; like the beavers even now at work in my backyard, we've rearranged things wherever we've lived. We've leveled the spots where we built our homes, cleared the forests for our fields, often fouled the nearby waters with our waste. That's just life. But this is different. In the last ten or twenty or thirty years, our impact has grown so much that we're changing even those places we don't inhabit: changing the way the weather works, changing the plants and animals that live at the poles and deep in the jungle. This is total. Of all the remarkable and unexpected things we've ever done as a species, this may be the biggest. Our new storms and new oceans and new glaciers and new springtimes—these are the eighth and ninth and tenth and eleventh wonders of the modern world, and we have lots more where those came from.

We have gotten very large, and the warm shadow that we cast falls across a different earth. We can't make the shadow disappear; for the foreseeable future we're stuck with it. The glaciers won't grow back again anytime soon, the oceans won't drop; we've already done deep and systemic damage. To use an intimate analogy, we've already said the angry and unforgivable words that will haunt our marriage till its end. And yet we can't simply walk out the door. There's no place to run. We have to salvage what we can of our relationship with the earth, keep things from getting any worse than they have to be.

And if we can bring our various emissions under sharp and quick control, we *can* limit the damage, reduce dramatically the chance of horrible surprises, preserve more semblance of the biology we were born into. But do not underestimate the enormity of the task: the U.N. estimates that we'd need an immediate 60 percent reduction in fossil-fuel use just to stabilize climate at the current level of disruption.[50] Nature may still meet us halfway, but halfway is a long way from where we are now. What's more, our retreat can't be put off. If we wait a few decades to really get started, we might as well not even begin. It's not a test, like poverty, that's always there for civilizations to address; it's a timed test, like the SATs. Two or three decades and then you lay your pencils down. It's *the* test for our generation, and population is a part of the answer.

chapter five

WHEN WE THINK ABOUT OVERPOPULATION, WE USUALLY THINK FIRST OF THE DEVELOPING WORLD, BECAUSE THAT'S WHERE 90 percent of new humans will be added during this final doubling. In *The Population Bomb*, the 1968 book that revived the Malthusian debate, Paul Ehrlich wrote that he hadn't understood the issue *emotionally* until he traveled to New Delhi, until he climbed into an ancient taxi hopping with fleas for the trip to his hotel. "As we crawled through the city, we entered a crowded slum area . . . the streets seemed alive with people. People eating, people washing, people sleeping. People visiting, arguing, and screaming. . . . People, people, people, people."[1]

But as Harvard's Amartya Sen points out, we fool ourselves when we think of population as a brown problem. The white world simply went through *its* population boom a century earlier (when Dickens was writing the same kind of descriptions of London). If the U.N. calculations are correct, and Asians and Africans make up just under 80 percent of humanity by 2050, then they would simply have returned "to being proportionately almost exactly as numerous as they were before the Industrial Revolution."[2]

And of course, Asians and Africans and Latin Americans are much smaller human beings, in the sense that we've been using the term—the balloon that floats above their heads is tiny in comparison with ours. Everyone has heard the statistics time and again, usually used in an attempt to make us feel guilty. But hear them one more time, with an open mind, simply trying to think strategically about how we will stave off the dangers to this planet. Pretend it's not a moral problem, just a mathematical one:

- An American uses seventy times the energy of a Bangladeshi, fifty times that of a Malagasy, twenty times that of a Costa Rican.[3]
- Since we live longer, the effect of each of us is further multiplied. In a year, an American uses three hundred times the energy of a Malian; over a lifetime, we'll actually use five hundred times as much.[4]
- Even if you factor in all other effects—such as the burning of forests—and attribute them to poor peasants, those who live in the poor world are typically responsible for the release of half a ton of carbon annually, compared with an average 3.5 tons for each resident of the "consumer nations" of western Europe and North America. The richest tenth of Americans—the people most likely to be reading this book—each emit eleven tons of carbon annually.[5]
- During the next decade India and China will each add to the planet about ten times as many people as will the United

States—but the stress on the natural world caused by those new Americans may exceed that from the new Indians and Chinese combined.[6] The 57.5 million northerners expected to be added during this decade will add more greenhouse gases to the atmosphere than the roughly 900 million southerners.[7]

These statistics are not eternal. Though inequality between north and south has steadily increased, the economies of the poor nations are now growing faster than those of the West. Sometime early in the twenty-first century China will pass the United States as the single largest source of carbon dioxide in the atmosphere, though of course it will be nowhere near the West on a per capita basis.[8]

For the moment, though (and it is the moment that counts), the United States is in a real sense the most populous nation on earth, and the one with the highest rate of growth. Though we only add about 3 million souls a year through both births and immigration, those new Americans are on average forty or fifty times the size of people born in the Third World. My daughter, four at this writing, has already used more stuff, added more waste to the environment, than most of the world's residents in a lifetime. In my thirty-six years, I've probably outdone small Indian villages.

Population growth in Rwanda, in Sudan, in El Salvador, in the slums of Lagos, in the highland hamlets of Chile can devastate *those places*. Growing too fast may mean that they run short of cropland to feed themselves and start planting erodible hillsides, of firewood to cook their food, of school desks and hospital beds. But population growth in those places doesn't devastate *the planet*. By contrast, we seem easily to absorb the modest annual increases in our population; in terms of our daily lives America seems only a little more crowded with each passing decade. You can still find a parking spot. But the earth simply can't absorb what we are adding to its saturated sinks.

• • •

So if it's "us," at least as much as "them," that need to bring this alteration of the earth under control, the question becomes, how? Many people who are sure that "controlling population" is the answer overseas are equally sure that there's a different answer here. If they are politicians and engineers, they're in favor of us living more *efficiently*—of building new cars that go much farther on a gallon of gas, or that don't use gas at all. If they're vegetarians, they support living more *simply*—riding bikes or buses instead of driving cars.

Both groups are utterly correct. I've spent much of my career writing about the need for cleverer technologies and more humble aspirations.[9] That's because environmental damage can be expressed as the sum of Population $\times$ Affluence $\times$ Technology. Surely the easiest solution would be to live more simply and more efficiently, and not worry too much about the number of people.

But I've come to believe that those changes in technology and in lifestyle are not going to happen easily and speedily; they'll be begun but not finished in the few decades that really matter. Remember that the pollution we're talking about is not precisely pollution, but rather things going the way they should—new filters on exhaust pipes won't do anything about that CO_2. We're stuck with making real changes in how we live. We're stuck with reducing dramatically the amount of fossil fuel we use. And since modern westerners are a kind of machine for burning fossil fuel, since virtually everything we do involves burning coal and gas and oil, since we're *wedded* to petroleum, it's going to be a messy breakup.

So we need to show, before returning again to population, why simplicity and efficiency won't save the day by themselves. And maybe the best place to start is with the career of President Clinton, in particular his reaction to global warming. Clinton is an exquisite scientific instrument, so finely tuned he can detect mood shifts in parts-per-million, a man whose career is built on his unparalleled ability to mirror public opinion. And on the one hand, he understands our predicament. Speaking to the United Nations early in the summer of 1997, he said quite plainly: "We humans are changing the global climate. . . . No nation can escape this danger. None can evade its responsibility to confront it, and we all must do our part."[10]

But when it's actually time to do our part, we don't. Clinton, after all, had first warned of the dangers of climate change in 1993, on his first Earth Day in office. In fact, he had solemnly promised to make sure America produced no more greenhouse gases in the year 2000 than it had in 1990, reaffirming a commitment President Bush had made the year before in Rio de Janeiro. But he didn't keep his word; in fact, the U.S. will spew an amazing 15 percent *more* carbon dioxide in 2000 than it did in 1990.[11] It's as if we'd promised the Russians we'd freeze our nuclear program and instead built a couple of thousand more warheads; we completely broke our word on what history may see as the most important international commitment of the 1990s.

What's important to understand is the reason *why* we broke our word. It's because Clinton understood that to keep this promise we would need to raise the price of fossil fuel. If gasoline cost $2.50 a gallon, we'd drive smaller cars, we'd drive electric cars, we'd take buses—and we'd elect a new president. Clinton made one feeble attempt to slightly raise the cost of oil with the so-called BTU tax he proposed in his freshman year, and he was roundly attacked from the right and the left. Some said the tax would cripple economic growth, while others called it a regressive levy harmful to the poor. So the president walked away from the issue. In fact, he crawled away from it: during the 1996 presidential election the price of gasoline spiked slightly higher, up to about $1.35 a gallon. President Clinton immediately offered to open the Strategic Petroleum Reserve—our stocks in event of national emergency—in order to keep the price of gas so low that no voter need think twice about filling up.

And you can hardly blame him, or any other politician. His real goal has been to speed the pace of economic growth, which has been the key to his popularity. If you could gather all world leaders into a single room, the one thing that every last socialist, Republican, Tory, monarchist, and trade unionist could agree on was Clinton's original campaign theme: "It's the economy, stupid." We've come to idolize economic growth. Turn on the evening news tonight. Anchormen who would never dream of backing one party or the other will gaze doe-eyed at the camera and say: "Good news today from the Commerce Department: the gross national product has grown at an annual rate of 4.5 percent." And of course, in some ways it is good news. Not only does it mean jobs for people, it means more money to do useful things, even some environmental things: the air over L.A. is cleaner than the air over Bangkok because we have the cash for catalytic converters. We've made great strides against air and water pollution in the last few decades even as our population and our economy have grown.

But the anchorman could just as easily say: "Sobering news tonight from the Commerce Department: we bought 4.5 percent more stuff this quarter than we did a year ago." Because for this other type of pollution represented by carbon dioxide, growth has so far been a cause, not a solution. Build more stuff, sell more stuff—use more energy. The U.S. State Department had to send a letter to the United Nations explaining why we had broken our Rio promise to reduce greenhouse gas emissions: the first two reasons cited are "lower-than-expected fuel prices" and "strong economic growth."[12] Former Senator Tim Wirth, who served as the chief voice in the first Clinton administration for good environmental policies, put it quite nakedly: the United States would miss its emissions targets due to "more prolonged economic activity than expected."[13]

And we're not the only ones—the Japanese broke their promise on global warming, too,[14] and the Canadians, and most of the Europeans. The Australians have announced they're not interested in targets for reducing CO_2, fearing it could cost each Australian $7,000 in potential wealth.[15] The momentum of economic growth is staggering, dwarfing the speed with which population expands. It took from the beginning of human history to the year 1900 for the economy to reach $600 billion in size; now it grows that much every two years. According to one estimate, "unchecked, today's $16 trillion global economy may be five times bigger only one generation or so hence."[16] *The most fearsome environmental damage comes from things going as they're supposed to go,* just at much too high a level. Reducing that damage will mean, literally, an end to business as usual.

It's not just the abstract idea of growth that we adore, however; it's also all its individual components. Take cars, for instance. If America is going to do anything about really reducing the cloud of CO_2 it puffs each year, it will have to burn far less gasoline. Technology has helped us in the past; on average, an American car gets twice as many miles to the gallon now as it did at the time of the first oil shock. Unfortunately, due to population increases, longer commuting distances, a decline in carpooling, and so forth, we have twice as many cars, and we drive them twice as far, completely canceling out the gain from all that new technology.

We may get better cars yet. The hypercars that technological seer Amory Lovins has been working on, for instance, could conceivably get a hundred miles to the gallon.[17] I've driven General Motors' EV1 electric, which goes from 0 to 60 miles per hour in about six seconds with the throaty grumble of a laptop computer. But there's no guarantee anyone will buy them: in the first five months of leasing the new electrics, GM managed to find 176 customers in California and Arizona.[18] At the moment, the top ten most fuel-efficient cars in the nation account for less than 1 percent of sales,[19] and the average car now going to a junkyard has better gas mileage than the average car coming off the dealer's lot.[20]

Instead of Civics and Metros, we're buying Expeditions, Navigators, and Explorers. People who have never *seen* a dirt road are buying 4X4s. Mercedes last summer introduced its version of the sport utility, which promptly sold out around the country. "I've been in the car business for ten years and I've never seen anything like this," said one dealer.[21] Ford has just started selling a new "vehicle," the Crew Wagon, that's a foot *longer* than the Suburban, with a V10 engine. "If you happen to get in a crash with a car, you probably won't even feel it," said a company official. "That's a kind of comforting perspective."[22] With gas costing less in real terms than ever before, newspaper reporters have no trouble finding families like the McIntoshes, who ferry their four children around upstate New York in a *pair* of Suburbans. "It's big and has a lot of power," explains Mrs. McIntosh.[23] Says David Van Sickle of the American Automobile Association, the average family may soon have a car "for every purpose. There will be a family sedan for hauling the family around, a sport ute for climbing mountains, a sports car to go out and enjoy a fling in every once in a while."[24]

People drive farther (miles traveled grew by 2 percent in 1995) and they drive faster (the average ticketed speed along the New York State Thruway near my home went from 73 to 76 miles per hour between 1995 and 1996).[25] Engineers even design cars to rumble more loudly because people like the sound of excess power.[26] We don't like the sound of conversation, though—18 million jobs were created between 1980 and 1990, but 22 million people started commuting by car in the same period.[27] Only 5 percent of people get to work by bus or rail, down 35 percent since 1970.[28] In fact, buses roll so empty through the streets that one UC-Berkeley study found cars are more fuel-efficient in some places than buses.[29]

I'm not saying we should give up trying to change people's driving habits; I'm not saying it's hopeless. We will doubtless come up with new technologies that will help; if we would spend the money to make bus systems convenient, many more people would ride them. All I'm saying is that the momentum in the wrong direction is deep and powerful, and to think that *by themselves* such lifestyle and technological changes will stop the flow of carbon dioxide in time is romantic.

It's romantic because consumerism—consumption—is by now an ideology, nearly a faith. It's barely a choice; it's deep in our bones, the way that religion was deep in the bones of your average fourteenth-century peasant. What are our rites of passage, our markers of significance? McDonald's recently began marketing the first doll in its porcelain "Treats for Tots" collection—"With a smile on his face and a sparkle in his baby blue eyes, 'Eric' is having the time of his life. He's enjoying his very first order of french fries with Mom and Dad at McDonald's. What fun it is to nibble them one at a time!" With cotton-blend romper and sun hat, "an outstanding value at only $59.95."

And even as we're consuming at levels that would have stunned a medieval monarch, consuming more than any people in any place at any time, most of us don't feel particularly rich, which makes it still less likely we'll make huge changes. Partly, the anthropologists tell us, this is because "a person's sense of well-being depends less on the objective reality of material affluence than on how his or her position compares to the reference group."[30] And in a television-dominated nation, there's no chance that we might be unaware, even for a day, that someone has more somewhere else. Advertising never ceases, not in the airport or the supermarket or the school or on the Web. Soon, promises *Wired* magazine, "push media," Internet-type messages that come across our wristwatches or eyeglass lenses or pagers, will "penetrate environments that have, in the past, been media-free—work, church, the solitude of a country walk."[31] Where I live in the Adirondack Mountains we're surrounded by wild places, lakes, rivers; life can be very sweet. But increasingly my neighbors, especially the kids, live in the generic suburbia of the tube and feel its pull, like salmon tugged upstream by some primal urge. The same signals go out around the world. *Baywatch*, a particular fantasy about a certain American way of life, reaches 1 billion humans a week, more than any cultural artifact since the birth of man.[32] In Thailand, 98 percent of teenagers are regular fans of MTV. "It's an all-news bulletin for creating brand images," enthused one multinational's "director of consumer intelligence."[33]

It is vital that we break out of this enchantment, and occasionally there are hopeful signs. When Joseph Dominguez and Vicki Robin wrote *Your Money or Your Life* a few years ago, it sold more than 600,000 copies, even though they urged readers to take it out of the library. The book, a guide to simplifying your life so you can reduce your expenses and work at the things that really matter to you, is radical—the authors lived on $6,000 a year, comfortably and happily. And it helped ignite an interest in "voluntary simplicity" that is still growing. "Every discipline, every sector of society is engaged in this shift away from excess and back to balance," writes Robin, who cites a recent *U.S. News & World Report* survey showing 48 percent of Americans had taken steps in the last five years to simplify their lives, and 51 percent said they wanted more free time even if it meant less money. "The time is ripe for turning the tide of overconsumption."[34] It's not an impossible sell, an unreachable ideal; as the Center for a New American Dream points out, by every measure our tremendous increase in possessions in the last five decades has not made us any happier.[35]

And yet, for the near future, don't count on the new simplicity alone to make a huge dent in any of the indicators that need denting—the amount of carbon dioxide pouring into the atmosphere, for instance. *Consumerism is in our bones.* "Hermès has a waiting list for its $4,000 Kelly bags. Neiman Marcus sold all fifty of the $75,000 Jaguars featured in its Christmas catalogue in eight days. Patek Philippe has back orders for a $44,500 watch." Sales of luxury goods, in fact, are growing faster even than sales of goods and services as a whole. True, says Isaac Lagnado, publisher of *Tactical Retail Monitor*, there was a brief period of austerity after the excesses of the 1980s.

"But memories are short and consumer confidence has rebounded. People are in the mood to spend."[36] Young bond traders crowd Manhattan showrooms to "finger the buttery leather seats" of a Ferrari Mondial, or rent a summer home for $70,000.[37] Baby boomers have more discretionary income than ever, now that their children are mostly grown, making them more likely to spend money on themselves. In the words of one expert, "How is a person going to say 'I can't afford that' when his portfolio has doubled in value in the last two years."[38] As boomers send their children off to college, they now routinely buy or build *bigger* homes, according to one survey of developers. By the year 2000, the average American home will be 2,500 square feet in size, up from 1,900 square feet in 1977.[39] We just keep getting larger.

Even our idea of "the simple life" often means little more than a shift in how we consume: country homes, "natural" cosmetics, organic this-and-that. Maybe you could take the kids out to dinner at a Rainforest Café, one of the country's fastest-growing restaurant chains, where animatronic trees talk to you through an artificial mist. When diners arrive, they are given a name for their adventure: "Viper, party of six," say. Then they wait in a rainforest retail store, examining "Sounds of the Rainforest" compact discs, until their table is called and they are led to their own corner of the mock jungle, complete with thunder, lightning, and robot apes. The company doesn't donate money from profits ($15.7 million in a recent quarter) to help save the actual rainforest, but it does contribute several thousand dollars a year that patrons toss into wishing wells. "We're in this for business purposes," says the chain's president. "We call it the three E's—entertainment, environment, and earning a return on investment."[40]

Changing the ways we live has to be a key part of dealing

with these new environmental dilemmas, if only because it is impossible to imagine a world where all 10 billion people consume at our levels. All I'm saying is, as we calculate what must happen over the next few decades to stanch the flow of CO_2, don't count on a conversion to simpler ways of life doing the trick *by itself*. Don't try to calculate carrying capacity for saints; an awful lot of angels could dance on the earth without doing much damage, but we're not angels. You'd think offhand that compared to changing fertility—the number of kids we bear— changing consumption patterns would be a breeze. Fertility, after all, seems *biological*—hard-wired into us in deep Darwinian ways. But in fact, I would guess that it's easier to change fertility than lifestyle. For better or for worse, we live in a culture that can say "that's enough" in regard to children at least as easily as it can regarding cars.

•   •   •

But perhaps our salvation lies in the other part of the equation, in the new technologies, new efficiencies, that could make even our wasteful lives benign and make moot the issue of our population. We are, for instance, converting our economy from its old industrial base to a new model based on service and information, and surely that should save some energy, should reduce the clouds of carbon. Writing software, after all, seems no more likely to damage the atmosphere than writing poetry.

Forget for a moment the hardware requirements of that new economy (a six-inch silicon wafer may require 3,000 gallons of water to produce, for instance);[41] just keep in mind that even a hospital or an insurance company or a basketball team requires a substantial physical base. Even the highest-tech office is built with steel and cement; it's filled with pipes and wires. And the money that's earned by people working in services will be spent on all sorts of things—more software, sure, but also more sport utility vehicles. As Department of Energy economist Arthur Rypinski says, "the information age has arrived, but even so people still get hot in the summer and cold in the winter. And even in the information age it tends to get dark."[42]

It's true that when it gets dark you could turn on a compact fluorescent bulb, saving half the energy of a regular incandescent. Indeed, the average American household, pushed and prodded by utilities and environmentalists, has in fact installed one compact fluorescent bulb over the last decade; unfortunately, over the same period, they've also added seven regular bulbs to the average home.[43] Millions of those halogen torchère lamps that throw their light up at the ceiling have been sold in recent years, mainly because they're $15.99 at Kmart. They also suck down electricity; those lamps alone have wiped out all the gains from the compact fluorescent bulbs. Since 1983 our energy use per capita has been increasing by almost 1 percent annually, despite all the technological advances of those years.[44]

As with our homes, so with our industries. Mobil Oil regularly buys ads in leading newspapers to tell "its side" of the environmental story. As they pointed out recently, between 1979 and 1993, "energy consumption per unit of gross domestic product" dropped 19 percent across the western nations. Which sounds good—it's better than 1 percent a year. But of course the GNP grew more than 2 percent annually. So total energy use, and total clouds of CO_2, continued to increase.[45]

It's not just that we use more, though. There are also more of us all the time, even in the United States. If the population is growing about 1 percent a year, then we have to keep increasing the efficiencies of our technology that much each year—and holding steady our standards of living—just to run in place. The President's Council on Sustainable Development, in its little-read report issued in the winter of 1996, concluded that "efficiency in the use of all resources would have to increase by more than fifty percent over the next four or five decades just to keep pace with population growth."[46] Three million new Americans annually means that many more cars, houses, refrigerators. Even if everyone consumes only what they consumed the year before, each year's tally of births and immigrants swells American consumption 1 percent.

It's against that tide that we demand the engineers and scientists swim. And it's a tide that turns into a wave if we imagine the rest of the world even trying to live in our fashion. It's true that the average resident of Shanghai or Bombay will not consume as lavishly as the typical San Diegan or Bostonian anytime soon, but they will make big gains, pumping that much more carbon into the atmosphere and requiring that we cut our own production even more sharply if we are to stabilize the world's climate.

The United Nations issued its omnibus report on sustainable development in 1987. Chaired by Norwegian prime minister Gro Harlem Brundtland, an international panel concluded that the world's economy would need to grow five to ten times larger to meet the needs of the poor world. And that growth won't mainly be in software. As the Department of Energy's Arthur Rypinski points out, "where the economy is growing really rapidly, energy use is too." In Thailand, in Tijuana, in Tanzania, every 10 percent increase in economic output requires 10 percent more fuel. "In the Far East the transition is from walking and bullocks to cars. People start out with electric lights and move on to lots of other stuff. Refrigerators are one of those things that are really popular everywhere. Practically no one, with the possible exception of people in the high Arctic, doesn't want a refrigerator. As people get wealthier they tend to like space heating and cooling, depending on the climate."[47]

In other words, if you're doing the math about how we're going to get out of this fix, you better figure in some unstoppable momentum in the rest of the planet from people who want the very basics of what we call a decent life. Even if we airlift solar collectors into China and India—which we should—those nations will still be burning more coal and oil. "What you can do with energy conservation in those situations is sort of at the margin," says Rypinski. "They're not interested in $15,000 clean cars versus $5,000 dirty cars. It was hard enough to get Americans to invest in efficiency; there's no feasible amount of largesse we can provide to the rest of the world to bring it about."[48]

In point of fact, we're doing just the opposite. What kind of car are we trying to introduce in China, for example? Electric vehicles? Natural gas? Hydrogen? Not quite. In March of 1997, vice president Al Gore saluted a joint venture between GM and a Shanghai firm to build—Buick Regals and Centurys. A Regal weighs 3,000 pounds and on city streets travels nineteen miles on a gallon of gas.[49] Whenever American officials take trade delegations off to China, they bring along the American manufacturers of power plants, boilers, turbines. Forget solar power—these generating stations are designed to use coal, of which China boasts half the world's supply. China plans to triple its coal production in the next two decades, and coal is the fuel source that produces the most carbon dioxide. Carbon emissions from powering Chinese refrigerators *alone* increased from 25.6 million tons in 1985 to an estimated 558 million tons in the year 2000. "You can't tell the people of Beijing that they can't buy a car or an air-conditioner because of the global climate-change issue," said Li Junfeng, a senior energy researcher for the State Planning Commission in Beijing. "It's just as hot in Beijing as it is in Washington, D.C." The most the experts dare hope is that China will only double, not treble, its output of CO_2 in the next thirty years. Even that, they stress, "would require a huge mobilization of capital, technology, and political commitment."[50] Instead, the chairman of Exxon recently went to Beijing to urge developing nations to avoid environmental controls that would hinder their development. "The earth's temperature often changes," he said, citing the Ice Ages as an example.[51]

The numbers are so daunting they're hard to imagine. Say, just for argument's sake, that we decided to cut world fossil-fuel use 60 percent, the amount that scientists say would stabilize world climate. And then say we shared that fossil fuel equally. Each human would get to produce 1.69 metric tons of carbon dioxide annually. Which would allow us to drive the average American car nine miles a day. By the time the population increases to 8.5 billion, in about 2025, we'd be down to six miles a day. Of course, if you carpooled, you'd have about three pounds of CO_2 left in your daily ration, enough to run a highly efficient refrigerator. Forget your computer, your TV, your stereo, your stove, your dishwasher, your water heater, your microwave, your water pump, your clock. Forget your light bulbs, compact fluorescent or not.[52]

I'm not trying to say that conservation, efficiency, and new technology won't help. They will help—but it will be slow and expensive. The tremendous momentum of growth will work against it. Say someone invented a new furnace tomorrow that used half the oil of old furnaces. How many years would it be before a substantial percentage of American homes were retrofitted with the new device? And if it cost more? And if oil stays dirt cheap? Changing basic fuels—to hydrogen, say—would be even more expensive. It's not like running out of white wine and switching to red. Arizona—the sunniest place on our continent—recently passed a landmark law insisting that *1 percent* of new electric generation come from solar power. Yes, we'll get new technologies. One day last fall *The New York Times* ran a special section on energy, featuring many up-and-coming improvements: solar shingles, basement fuel cells. But the same day, on the front page, William K. Stevens reported that international negotiators had all but given up on preventing a doubling of the atmospheric concentration of CO_2. The momentum of growth was so large that diplomats said the changes required to really slow global warming would be like "trying to turn a supertanker in a sea of syrup."[53]

That was the message that came through loud and clear at the Kyoto negotiations on global warming held in December 1997. Though in many ways a great achievement, the treaty produced at Kyoto came nowhere near reducing the amount of CO_2 flowing into the atmosphere. At most it will cut somewhat the emissions of the industrialized nations—and then only if it's ratified by the Senate, and if we pass the tough measures, like increased gas taxes, necessary to make it work. The Kyoto negotiations represent the very first admission from world leaders that perhaps the impact of our species has grown large enough, but that glimmer of recognition will take decades to grow into the foundation of policy.

There are no silver bullets against a problem this systemic. Electric cars won't save us by themselves, though they would help. We simply won't live efficiently enough soon enough to solve the problem. Vegetarianism won't cure our ills, though it would help. We simply won't live simply enough soon enough to solve the problem.

Reducing the birthrate won't end all our troubles either. It, too, is no silver bullet. It's just that it, too, would help.

• • •

Carl Haub stares into his computer at the Population Reference Bureau, punches in a few numbers, and sits back while the machine spews out projections. He can plug in any variables you like. Say, in the year 2000, American women began averaging 1.5 children apiece, down from about 2 at the moment. That would mean a large number of couples deciding to have a single child instead of two or three. And further, just for argument's sake, reduce by half the number of legal immigrants to the United States, allowing 400,000 annually—a painful subject we'll return to in greater detail later. What you get is a population that rises very gradually, plateaus in about 2020, and then gradually decreases to 230 million in 2050.[54] That compares with the Census Bureau's best guess that we'll be at 400 million Americans in 2050 if current trends hold.

That gap of 170 million Americans is not enough to change the basic outline of the world's predicament. We'd still be giving off more carbon than the earth's sinks can contain; China would still be growing; the planet would still be changing rapidly. But perhaps, especially if the countries of western Europe and Japan manage similar birthrates and see their populations begin to shrink slightly, too, it would open a little window for luck and ingenuity. We'd give ourselves a bit more margin. That's all this book is about. Not saving the world, simply opening up a little room for ingenuity and discipline and grace.

Even if we don't manage to drop our birthrates as far as I've proposed—even if our population grows to "only" 300 or 350 million instead of 400 million by the middle of the next century—that would *help*. It's all an enormous math problem, where some calculation of our numbers multiplied by our impact must balance against the capacities of the planet. Recycling your cans subtracts a tiny number from the equation; reproducing less fervently subtracts a much larger number. If we can cut the birthrate, that's 50 or 100 million fewer cars and furnaces; 50 or 100 million fewer dinners to serve and thermostats to set each day; 50 or 100 million fewer giant balloons hovering above the landscape.

Throughout this section I've concentrated on the effects of our predicament on our own species. But one could argue for these changes from many other directions. If the temperature goes up five degrees, for instance, half the states in the Union could lose their populations of trout and other cold-water fish; the sugar maple could disappear from America.[55] Already we take up so much of the planet, use so much of its bounty, that some biologists say large vertebrate evolution has come to an end; bears and elk and wolves lack the space to bounce off each other and continue the constant dance of change that has always marked their existence. Other scientists warn that the wave of extinctions caused by rapid global warming would be at least as extensive as during an ice age. I've written about these issues in the past, tried to explain my sense that a world where humans drive the most basic physical forces on the planet would be a sadder, lonelier world.[56]

But here I want to be as practical as possible, as fixated on people. There's no more practical decision than how many children to have. (And no more mystical decision either.) This is a basic bottom-line argument. The next fifty years are a special time. They will decide how strong and healthy the planet will be for centuries to come. Between now and 2050 we'll see the zenith, or very nearly, of human population; with luck we'll see the maximum production of carbon dioxide, of toxic chemicals. We'll see the peak of species extinction, of soil erosion. Greenpeace recently announced a campaign to phase out fossil fuels entirely by mid-century,[57] which sounds utterly quixotic now but could, if everything went just right, happen.

So it's the task of those of us alive right now to deal with this special phase, to squeeze us through these next fifty years. That's not fair, no more than it was fair that earlier generations had to deal with World War II or the Civil War or the Revolution, with the Depression or with slavery. It's just reality. We need, in these fifty years, to be working simultaneously on all parts of the equation—on our ways of life, on our technologies, and on our populations. We need to be electing the right politicians, boycotting the wrong companies, recycling, riding bikes, buying tiny little cars. *If we can open up a bit more margin by having fewer kids, that will help.* It's like trying to make sure your car has 60,000 miles instead of 90,000 a decade after you got it. It's still not a new car. The difference between 60,000 and 90,000 is subtle. But it's real, too.

You may well ask, "Why have any children at all?" Wouldn't it be better still to have none? I know several people who have made that decision—Stephanie Mills, for instance, a fine environmental writer, who declared in her college commencement address two decades ago that she would bear no children. (There are others, less thoughtful; one recent letter to the editor in a nature magazine concluded, "I say that if you have children, you are not an environmentalist."[58] A month later someone else wrote in to second the motion, adding "for those who have strong maternal or paternal feelings, how about adopting a homeless companion animal?"[59]) Indeed, it's a question Sue and I asked ourselves many times. When I was writing *The End of Nature*, I said, ambiguously, that we were trying "very hard not to think about how much we'd like a baby."[60]

What eventually made up our minds was largely simple desire; like most, though certainly not all, people we felt some need deeper than deep to raise and nurture a child. Anything else may simply be justification. But we also sensed something that I've been trying to say throughout this book: that our lifetime actually did fall at a special moment, and not just for the physical reasons I've already discussed. It seems special in almost an emotional sense—it's a point in time poised uniquely between hope and fear. It is possible that we face unavoidable calamity, but it's also possible that we'll see remarkable change. Every week brings news of technical innovation, and there are brief shows of political will—at least our leaders feel the need to talk about issues like global warming, even if their talk so far amounts to little. More encouraging, in the last ten years growing numbers of people have started to sense they want something different out of life; their searching is not yet a movement to rival the consumerism reshaping the planet, but at least it's a detectable motion beneath the surface of the culture. I've been to places in the last ten years that seem to me to offer actual alternative visions of what we might become: cities where buses have replaced cars to general delight, a few poor nations where education and health are flourishing without the overdevelopment that marks our civilization. Though dark in many ways, it is not a hopeless world our Sophie was born into. It's not a guaranteed world, either—it's poised somewhere in between.

A quarter-century from now, when Sophie's likely to be thinking about children, it may be easier to tell if our societies waited too late to change, if we really are heading for the various hells the "overshoot" theorists warn us about. Fifty years from now the equations may have changed altogether. We may be in more desperate straits, as weird weather cuts crop yields and rising sea levels require huge efforts to protect our cities. Or we may have turned certain corners: we may ride buses and bikes and drive hydrogen cars; carbon levels may be falling in the atmosphere; climate may be stabilizing. It may make sense, from the planet's standpoint, to think of two kids as normal again; perhaps the day will come when our technologies and our ways of life are so subtle and unassuming that we can double our population once more. But for now, for us, one seems right.

As Gregg Easterbrook points out in his book *A Moment on the Earth*, if the planet does manage to reduce its fertility, "the period in which human numbers threaten the biosphere on a general scale will turn out to have been much, much more brief" than periods of natural threats like ice ages.[61] True enough. It's just that the period in question happens to be our time. It's what makes this moment special, and what makes this moment hard.

PART THREE

NATION

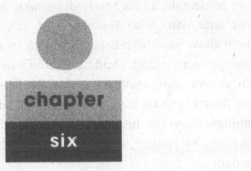

chapter

six

IN A WEEDY GROVE ON THE EAST SIDE OF THE SACANDAGA RIVER, WHERE THE BLACKSMITH MUST HAVE HAD HIS FORGE, I FOUND horseshoes, hinges, angles, corners, chains, flanges—all the essentials of the early Industrial Revolution, rust flaking off them in brown sheets. Across the river an iron ring still clung firmly to a granite ledge; it must have once secured a guy wire for a big chimney. An old woodstove with all the fancy iron-work stood under a birch tree, berry cane growing up through the belly. It's mostly blackberry there now, and birch and hemlock, with just the odd topography of old cellar holes remaining to mark the factory and the town. Deer scat, trillium, barrel hoops.

Griffin, this old ghost town, lies maybe eight miles from my house if you go by foot across the mountains. It's not a picturesque ghost town like you'd find in Arizona. Here in the Adirondacks a century of humidity, of snow and rain, of trees grown big with roots strong enough to crack stone, has turned the settlement into a barely discernible memory. If you walk the land with John Teachout, the sole remaining resident, he'll show you the cellars, each with its own well, hand-dug and perfectly round. (And he'll show you his own well, with a trout swimming cramped circles, keeping it nice and clean.) He'll show you where the hotel stood, and the school; with his guidance you can just about imagine it all. But if you walked the land by yourself, you'd more or less think you were in the woods.

Which is not to say that Griffin left no trace. John Teachout can also show you pictures—photographs that his father left him. He sits at the picnic table in his dooryard (next to the shed with the neatly lettered sign that reads: IF YOU WANT TO BREAK INTO MY CAMP, LET ME GIVE YOU FAIR WARNING. IS WHAT YOU FIND INSIDE WORTH DYING OVER??? THINK ABOUT IT!!!) and flips the photos to you, one by one, pausing now and then to roll a cigarette from a store of tobacco he keeps in a cookie tin. Here's a picture of some serious-faced men at the mill, and here's one of twenty-seven kids on the schoolhouse steps, they, too, wearing the grim looks with which the nineteenth century faced the camera. "This one's from around 1900—already you can see the mill falling in," says Teachout.

We know about this town not just from old photos but also from the work of several historians. Barbara McMartin, the preeminent chronicler of the Adirondack woods, has written about life in these hamlets, which were built on hemlock—on the tannin in the bark of the hemlock, to be precise, which for a while cured the gloves of half the world. First men felled the trees, peeling off the bark in foot-wide strips and leaving the trunks to rot; horses pulled the bark to the nearest roads, where it was piled and left for the huge wagons or sledges that carried them to the tanneries. Not all who drove them were men; one local history recalls a single mother, Emeline Brace, with a team of black horses, who hauled bark. She had no one to leave her fifteen-month-old baby with, so she made a wooden box for him, filled with blankets and straw, and bored two or three holes in the side so he could have fresh air to breathe but not freeze in the 30-below mornings.

Stephen Griffin, for whom this place was named, controlled 30,000 acres; his was one of the nation's largest operations. We can guess about his employees, the men who ran the bark grinders (which left a haze of highly flammable hemlock dust floating through the dark workshops) and the machines that agitated the dry hides as they were being soaked for tanning. Most of the men were French-Canadian or Irish; for a month of twelve-hour days, they might have made $35. Rent in the company houses was 50 cents a week. "After the hides were tanned, men with iron hooks would pull them out of the vats and throw them over large poles to dry," recalled one witness. "No one except an experienced man could pull hide out of a vat and throw it over one of these poles that was as high as a man's head. If you were to stand and watch one of these Irishmen pull one of those wet heavy hides out of this hot liquor, you would say there was nothing to it. But let someone try it who did not know how. He wouldn't be able to throw a hide over the pole in half an hour, and I dare say he would give up trying."[1]

Some of the people who lived in Griffin when it boomed set down their memories in writing. So we know, for instance, that Myra Girard taught for two terms in the little schoolhouse and the thing that she remembered best was the day a "hurricane" came from the west. "It tore the roof off the woodshed and threw it clear over the schoolhouse. She got under her desk and the children got under their desks, not knowing what was going to happen next. Then it calmed down." We know that when Henry Girard wanted to marry Nellie McCarthy he sent to Glens Falls for a wedding ring, but that the mailbag was carelessly tossed out at North Creek and landed in front of the train's wheels, which flattened the ring completely. (The railroad paid for a new one, and it got there in time for the wedding.) We know that sometimes everyone would pitch in and hire a band from Northville, twenty-three miles away, to come play at a celebration, and that one time a group of lumberjacks who were listening to the music "started boxing, which was quite a hobby in those days. When they stopped playing all the men stopped boxing; when they started playing again most of the lumbermen started boxing again. The musicians had a hard time to keep from laughing."[2]

And we know this, too: at the end of the nineteenth century some scientist figured out a synthetic process for tanning hides and so the hemlock bark was no longer needed. The mills caved in or burned down. The people moved away. Not just from Griffin, but from Arietta, Jerden Falls, from the town of Oregon. The small hamlet where I live, Johnsburg, once bustled—twenty-three mills took advantage of the hydropower pouring down Mill Creek. Now there's not one mill left and people are starting again to call the stream Beaver Brook, the name the first settlers had given to it. Far fewer people live in Johnsburg than lived here a century ago, and far fewer cattle and sheep. I know a man who can remember when most of the land around town was cleared for pasture, when "you couldn't step out your door without hearing the dingle of a cow bell."[3] But the milk business changed, too; the big dairies put the mountain herds out of business, and now the trees have grown in so thick that it's hard to find a cleared piece of land big enough for a game of catch.

We need in this section to talk about economics and national security and Social Security and demographics and immigration—talk about them at some length, and with some unavoidable abstraction. These are things that would inevitably be affected if many of us decided to have smaller families. They are crucial to this argument, even if only to answer the logical and obvious objections to such a shift. But before we get to those pragmatic questions, I think, we need to deal with the intuitive fear of getting smaller, of *decline*. Of the human mark receding from certain places, as it will certainly recede if our population shrinks somewhat. That's why I've begun with these shards of local history.

This fear of decline comes from an old place inside us, so old that it's hard to pull out and examine, except to say that an abandoned cellar hole with a birch tree growing up out the middle of it gives many people the willies. Michael Pollan, in his book *Second Nature*, describes coming across the ruins of an old farming village, Dudleytown, near his Connecticut retreat: "It is a spooky place. I'm not talking only about the ghostliness of an abandoned settlement, or the weight of the past one often feels among ruins. What makes Dudleytown spooky is the evident speed and force and thoroughness with which the forest has obliterated the place. In the space of a few decades it has erased virtually every human mark."[4] He returns home to tend his garden, determined to keep Dudleytown and all that it represents at bay.

John Stilgoe, a Harvard professor who has spent much of his career crisscrossing the country to study such places, says Pollan is not alone. "The more educated people are, the spookier they find such ruins," he says. "For people who worship a god called Progress, such places are a confession of failure. Here is a place where people spent a lot of time and energy and it didn't work out. So maybe what we're doing is going to fail too. When they come up against a landscape that's failed, they can't bring themselves to look at it."

But that spookiness rarely haunts me anymore, certainly not on this blue-sky spring day in Griffin, standing on the bridge over the Sacandaga, hearing the snowmelt roar as it pounds south through the little gorge. The human presence here was good—not environmentally benign by our current standards, not safe in the way an OSHA inspector would calculate it, not particularly cultured. But good—filled with love, hard work, fistfights, trout dinners, and the other things that make us human. *And the forest that fills in the cellar holes is good, too.*

It's not a failure, it's a change. First one thing was here, and now something else has come, or come back. The last moose was spotted in Griffin in 1852, and the boy who saw it was scared enough by the sight of those big antlers that he lay down in the dry creek bed and hid. Now, 146 years later, the woods are back and so is the moose—I saw droppings the size of Ping-Pong balls, and that cloven track pressed deep in the mud.

It's a complicated business, deciding to get smaller. But if we took up a little less space, the rest of creation would expand to fill that gap. And if we did it *confidently*, if we *chose* to, then there might be something kind of lovely about it.

• • •

We are a species like all others, bent on survival. And even when we had made ourselves reasonably secure against other animals, we had our own kind to fear. So the time-honored reason for any society to fear getting smaller, beyond the intuitive worry about simply shrinking away, is the sense that it would simultaneously grow weak, unable to confront its enemies. "Lots of them" and "few of us" long equaled annihilation or assimilation.

In recent centuries, in the western world, the most eloquent worriers on this topic have been the French, probably because they shared a border with the more robust Germans. As early as 1871, when Bismarck won the Franco-Prussian War, influential Catholic leaders saw the nation's defeats as signs "of divine chastisement of the French people for the sin of contraception."[5] But it was not just conservatives and clerics who fretted. Émile Zola, the great novelist and great republican, helped found the National Alliance for the Growth of the French Population in the 1890s, and wrote his last novel, *Fécondité*, to promote the cause. It contrasted the dissolute (and contracepting) lifestyles of the urban and rural bourgeoisie with a peasant couple notable for their healthy good cheer and their diligent childbearing (at one point in the middle of the novel, Marianne delivers at the rate of one child every two pages). By book's end, each of the tiny families of the elite has died out, but 158 descendants of Marianne and Matthieu assemble on their farm to celebrate their seventieth anniversary. "We shall swarm and fill the world!" cries one.[6]

Though France held Verdun and Germany lost the war of attrition on the Western Front, the fears only heated up after World War I. Georges Clemenceau, debating the Versailles Treaty, declared, "The treaty does not say that France must undertake to have children, but that is the first thing which ought to have been put into it." But not just the French. The English worried that Russian numbers were growing too fast; Stalin, meanwhile, was so spooked by a decline in Russian birthrates that he banned abortion and taxed celibates, childless couples, and those with only one child.[7] From the beginning of birth control to the end of World War II, people believed wholeheartedly in a kind of demographic determinism, and the fight against Hitler seemed to justify all the hysteria—it was only the vast pools of people in the United States and especially the Soviet Union that turned the tide.

But the end of the war, and the dropping of the atom bomb, signaled a new moment, a new mathematics. In the postmodern military age, technical savvy and economic power became at least as important as cannon fodder. We may not be able to fight the same kind of wars—Edward Luttwak, a former Reagan policy adviser, wrote in *Foreign Affairs* that in the days of large families "a death in combat was not the extraordinary and fundamentally unacceptable event that it is now"[8]—but that's nothing to mourn. If we have to defend ourselves, we can do so with the expensive weaponry we've spent the last few decades buying and building.

If there is, God forbid, a World War III, it won't look like the last two. And meanwhile, what forces are most likely to cause anger and strife around the world? Not only the usual assortment of religious and ethnic hatreds, not just the gaps between rich and poor, but also the precise kind of environmental pressures that I've already described: the growing shortages of water and perhaps food, the waves of "environmental refugees" likely to be set loose by deforestation and desertification and rising sea levels. The British researcher Norman Myers calculates that by the time the greenhouse effect is in full swing, perhaps one human in fifty will be an "environmental refugee," forming what the Aga Khan once called "a perfect recipe for widespread human suffering, social disorder, and political instability."[9]

If it's the last war you want to fight, in other words, then we need more babies; if it's the next war you want to prevent, then fewer might help.

•   •   •

But fewer babies might trigger other problems; a stable population is such a new idea that it will doubtless come with ramifications, including changes in the economy. One big reason, after all, that our economies keep growing is that our numbers keep growing; it doesn't take any special genius to see that if there are 3 million more Americans next year, the demand for refrigerators, underwear, new houses, light bulbs, and every other staple commodity will also grow. One percent more Americans means 1 percent more American teeth, which means 1 percent more toothpaste.

And so a stable, or even slowly declining, number of Americans means a very different, probably less gung-ho economy—a third or more of our economic growth in recent decades merely reflected our continuing growth in population. As Ben Wattenberg points out, without continued rapid growth "that escalator of consumer demand won't continue."[10] But no one can predict all the impacts with any certainty. For instance, the asset value of people's homes might fall as demand for housing shrank; on the other hand, the amount of money it took for a young family to buy a house would likely fall as well. There might be fewer jobs, but of course there'd be fewer workers competing for them. Population growth, as Julian Simon and Karl Zinsmeister pointed out in a recent essay, can help the economy because people work harder to support their kids, because it reduces the risk of expansion, and because it promotes economies of scale.[11] Or, as a 1958 issue of *Life* put it, "Kids—A Built-in Recession Cure. How 4,000,000 a Year Make Millions in Business."[12] And our growth tends to pull other nations along. A gathering of demographers at the U.N. last fall worried that stable populations in the developed world would not import enough from

Asia and Latin America, leading to a "global readjustment."[13]

But true as those fears may be, they do not solve the question. We tend, in this society, to rank economic issues above all others. If something might slow the economy, we won't even discuss it. But as I tried to show in my long examination of our current environmental predicament, the perpetual expansion in the size of our economies is at least as damaging as the expansion of our populations. If they can be stabilized in tandem, so much the better. A "global readjustment" of our economies, our expectations, is probably in order—sooner or later, our ceaseless growth will have to stop.

It's true that the maturing of our economies will no doubt feel weird at first. As Adam Smith himself said, "the progressive state is in reality the hearty state to all the different orders of society; the stationary is dull."[14] But he's really just guessing. We don't know what stability might feel like. Perhaps, like the end of any exuberant adolescence, it will be equal parts bitter and sweet.

As an example, let's look in depth at one of the few economic impacts of lower birthrates that we know enough about to discuss intelligently. The biggest effect on our society of a drop in fertility would be to make the nation slightly grayer around the temples. There would be fewer young people, and plenty of senior citizens; America would be "older."

This is happening already, of course. As the baby boom generation ages, and its members average about two children instead of about three, the percentage of older Americans (who are living ever longer) will increase. Even at current birthrates, the median age for Americans should increase from 34.6 years in 1996 to 38 years in 2050.[15] As former Commerce Secretary Pete Peterson points out, within a generation all of America will look the way Florida looks today, which is to say a little wrinkled under the tan.[16] And we are not alone; as birthrates around the world drop, every country on the planet will begin to experience an aging population. Some will be ahead of us—Japan, for instance, where there's a government ministry devoted to the "aging problem."

If you decrease both the birthrate and the immigration rate, as I've proposed, then this problem—if it is a problem— will get somewhat worse. According to Carl Haub of the Population Reference Bureau, if the average American woman were having 1.5 children, and the rate of immigration was 400,000 annually, then by 2050 just under one-quarter of Americans would be over sixty-five.[17]

Eventually, of course, we'll be in this situation no matter what we do, unless we unleash another baby boom of post–World War II magnitude. Some indeed have proposed such a plan. In eastern Germany they'll pay you $650 for giving birth; similar schemes exist in Belgium, Luxembourg, and Portugal. But even if we did that in the United States, ignoring every kind of environmental warning, we'd just postpone the reckoning. *Someday* the population will have to stabilize, and as it does, our average age will creep up. If you have a stable population that lives thirty years on average, then you can have a young society. But if you have a stable population where most people live to be eighty years old, it will by definition be much grayer. You can't have stability, youth, and long life expectancies all at the same time.

Viewed one way, of course, our aging population constitutes a wonderful achievement. If you were born in 1900, you could expect to live forty-seven years; if you were born in 1991, you could expect your life to last about seventy-five years. That's 60 percent longer, twenty-eight more years, 10,000 more sunrises and newspapers and glasses of orange juice. I know that quality counts more than quantity, that short lives can be filled with meaning and long ones full of nothing, but still this seems to me the most remarkable joy of living in the late twentieth century, far more profound than the car or the TV or our other marvels. We embrace these statistics for ourselves, for the people we love, indeed for just about every individual we can imagine—they've changed the way the world feels to us. We get twice the adult years we used to! Where I live, there are a lot of people *looking forward* to moving to Florida. And yet for that organism we call "society as a whole," the same facts make us somehow gloomy. This aging process, former Commerce Secretary Peterson suggests, "will challenge the very core of our national psyche, which has always been predicated on fresh beginnings, child-like optimism, and aspiring new generations."[18]

Which leaves us a choice: either we get an enormous bunch of new babies, and the generation after that an even more enormous bunch, and the generation after that a truly stupendous number until very rapidly we're as densely populated as India. Or we figure out new ways to think about ourselves and our nation that turn this demographic inevitability of aging from a disaster into a commonplace, a given, even a kind of gift. That's what the rest of this chapter is about: new ways of dealing with old age. It may seem infinitely far removed from the question of how many babies to bear, but in fact it is closely related. Not only will a society with a lower birthrate be older, but it is fears about about how we will fare as we age that have often motivated humans to reproduce. And our worries about our children as they grow old can lead us to want to give them siblings. You can't discuss fertility, in other words, without addressing mortality; the beginnings of our lives are chained to their ends in every way.

"We have met the financial 'enemy,' and he is the elderly 'us,'" writes MIT economist Lester Thurow in his book *The Future of Capitalism*.[19] It's hard to get much blunter than that. The elderly, he and other economists insist, will soon comprise "a large group of affluent, economically inactive, elderly voters who require expensive social services like health care and who depend upon government for much of their income." It is, insists Thurow, a "revolutionary class, one that is bringing down the welfare state, destroying government finances, altering the distribution of purchasing power, and threatening the investments that all societies need to make to have a successful future."[20] It sounds like a case only Dr. Kevorkian could solve.

So let's begin with the bottom line: will an aging society truly impoverish us? The argument is pretty clear, and it goes something like this: Old people are unproductive, and they demand government handouts, hence they're extremely expensive to keep around. The rest of us have to work ever harder to support them.

Like most caricatures, this argument contains a certain amount of truth, and like most caricatures it also hides a good deal. For instance, remember that as a society ages, and especially if more and more people are having a single child, the number of children it must take care of will shrink as the number of old people grows. The aging of the baby boomers, for instance, will mean we need many more nursing homes and gerontologists. But even at the height of their aging, the percentage of "dependent" people in the population will be about exactly the same as it was when they were born—when they needed nursery schools and pediatricians.[21] If and when the population stabilizes, neither growing nor shrinking, 39 percent of the people will either be young or old, precisely the percentage when John Kennedy was elected president.[22] The trade-off between kids and the elderly is not perfect; many studies indicate that children are less expensive to care for. On the other hand, many elderly people remain productive, working a part-time job or calling their broker at Fidelity, which is more than you can say for most five-year-olds.

Not only that, very few septuagenarians involve themselves in drive-by shootings, which is more than you can say for seventeen-year-olds. Although males aged fourteen to twenty-four make up just 8 percent of the population, they account for 48 percent of its murders;[23] a complete economic accounting would have to factor in the costs of crime, and of locks and alarms and guards and prisons. And it would have to include the productivity contributed by volunteers. As conservative economist Richard Posner points out, in the dense language of his tribe, "retirement causes people to increase their nonmarket production because the opportunity cost of that production—the income they would be earning in market production were they not retired—is now lower."[24] In other words, there may be a lot of old people getting taken care of in the hospital, but there are also a lot of old people sitting at the front desk taking calls.

Neither of my parents works any longer at a regular job. But my father just wrote his first book, a history of the Gillette Corporation published by the Harvard Business School Press. He's making money, as well as spreading ideas that will help others make money. And my mother tutors new arrivals to this country from eastern Europe and Southeast Asia; because they speak better English, they presumably make better money. Neither of my parents is ill, and neither to my knowledge has taken up serious crime to fill the hours left free by retirement. It is, in other words, difficult to calculate the extent to which they've become economic burdens; certainly, they are generous to their children and grandchildren. It's true that they may eventually require costly medical care, but as demographers Lincoln and Alice Day point out, it's not completely fair to attribute the cost of that care to an aging population. It's not growing old that's so expensive, their data show; it's dying. Since 85 percent of Americans now die after sixty-five, "this concentrates the costs of dying within old age and makes the young and middle-aged appear to be less of a financial drain."[25] It is, in other words, something of a statistical phantom.

But there is one thing that is beyond debate, both about my parents and about the elderly as a whole. Every month the government sends them checks. And as a population ages, there are going to be more and more of those checks arriving in mailboxes, and fewer and fewer people paying the payroll taxes that support them. If it's relatively impossible to calculate the costs of aging, it's relatively simple to calculate the costs of Social Security. Easy and a little frightening.

•   •   •

If you don't count payments on the national debt, half the federal budget goes to the elderly, a proportion that would rise to 100 percent sometime in the next century if the retirement laws remain unchanged.[26] Abroad, the situation is much the same—most nations would need a payroll tax increase of 15 to 20 percent to make their pension funds solvent.[27] Numbers like those have alarmed all sorts of commentators: these unfunded obligations are "an economic iceberg," posing "the greatest challenge to the United States in its history."[28] Even "Draconian budget cuts" offer "only a small amount of breathing room."[29] And by reducing the birthrate my proposals would add—if only a little—to this dilemma.

It's one of those crises that you can see coming a long ways away and that we so far seem powerless to stop. In part that's because the math is arcane and a little dull. (Though not to everyone. Former Commerce Secretary Peterson, in his manifesto on the subject, relates that "recently my fellow Nebraskan Warren Buffett shared with me his delightful tale of the Static Islanders, a small, isolated, and rapidly aging society." This delightful legend continues for several pages as the Static Islanders go about growing their rice and making their wine from "an abundant indigenous berry" until some iron laws about productivity expressed by the equation "66 workers $\times$ 13^1%$_5$ hours $\times$ 2 ounces hourly = 1800 ounces" remind them that "promises regarding future consumption must be constrained by a knowledge of demographics and realistic estimates of future production."[30]) Still, polls indicate a deeper belief in UFOs than in the chance today's workers will get back what they've paid into the system—most people seem to have gotten the message.

Before we get to what we might do, though, let me repeat once again what won't work: having more babies. To stabilize the ratio of retirees to workers, U.S. fertility would have to surge to a rate of three births per woman or higher.[31] Not only is that unlikely to happen, it also would produce a population the size of China's within a few generations. It's not *realistic*.

When reformers try to figure out what *is* realistic, they sometimes look to the past, to an age when families, not governments, took care of the aged. Among many other things, such informal support for the aged has the advantage of being cheap; your daughter doesn't charge Medicare $75 every time she changes the sheets. My grandmother lived with my family the last ten years of her life, and it was wonderful and it was hard and it cost the taxpayers a lot less than sticking her in the nursing home. Still, it's probably romantic to think such "kin networks" will provide more help in the future than they do now. As families get smaller, there are fewer children to change the sheets. And in any event, as certain core western values spread around the world, young people are becoming less interested in making anyone else's bed. Even in Asia, where Confucian devotion to filial piety runs deep (where even the 1954 Maoist constitution asserted that Chinese children "who have come of age have the duty to support and assist their parents"),[32] such attachments are fading. Nicholas Kristof, writing in *The New York Times*, reports that "a revolutionary shift in attitudes toward the elderly appears to be underway in Japan, and to some extent in Korea and China as well." Fifty percent of Japanese elderly still live with their children, but that number was 80 percent as recently as 1970. Among American elders, meanwhile, the percentage who want to live with their children is quite small. In one poll far more wanted to go to a nursing home than move in with their kids.[33]

So if we can't count on informal networks of support to provide for the aging, we will probably need to reform the various pension and social security systems that support most of the developed world's elderly. That's because they come with a built-in flaw. People don't really pay into a "fund" that saves their money for them until they retire; instead, these are pay-as-you-go systems, where the taxes of today's workers support today's retirees. This works enormously well when the population is growing; in the 1960s, at the height of the baby boom, the renowned economist Paul Samuelson wrote in *Newsweek* that "the beauty of social insurance is that it is actuarially unsound. Everyone who reaches retirement age is given benefit privileges that far exceed anything he has paid in. . . . How is this possible? . . . Always there are more youths than old folks in a growing population."[34] In fact, he continued, "a growing nation is the greatest Ponzi game ever contrived."[35] Around the developed world, in those palmy days, politicians turned what had been modest supplementary pension schemes into ever-more-lavish payouts. Richard Nixon raised benefits for American retirees by 20 percent across the board in 1972, and then he indexed them to inflation. But that was right about the moment that birthrates began to fall and inflation began to rise, and so pretty soon every government in the industrial world had a big new worry. There have been a few mild reforms since then (raising the retirement age from 65 to 67, for instance) but not enough to change the basic mathematics of the system.

One reform proposal after another has popped up in recent years. Almost no one simply proposes letting Americans decide on their own if they want to save for retirement, because it's clear they won't—the baby boomers are saving roughly one-third the amount they would need in order to have the standard of living in retirement that their parents enjoy.[36] But a growing number of libertarians want to privatize the whole system; your payroll taxes would be turned over to you to invest as you saw fit. If a twenty-five-year-old stuck her deductions in the stock market or found other high-return investments, according to one study by the Cato Institute, she might get three to six times more money back than if she left it in the giant Social Security strongbox.[37] Critics have pointed out a few flaws with the proposal, aside from the fact that it would make a mint for the Wall Street money managers now funding most of the think tanks and politicians pushing the idea.[38] For one thing, it's a little risky. It's true that the stock market has outperformed government bonds. But let's say people are shoveling vast sums into stocks and waiting for retirement. Even assuming the markets keep growing, what will happen when they start to retire? The first boomer may get his money out and profit handsomely, says Peterson. "But can seventy-six million Boomers?" The value of assets could suddenly depreciate dramatically, perhaps as much as 45 percent.[39]

Peterson believes that Americans must raise their savings rates, forgoing consumption in the hope that the country's productivity will be boosted over the long term. The government should make this easier, he says, by setting up various incentives to save, but it will mainly require a shift in mindset—only 20 percent of Americans are currently "planners" that save toward a quantitative goal. The rest—"strugglers," "impulsives," and "deniers"—"leave their future more or less to fate," some because they make so little money, more because they like to buy stuff. When Americans were surveyed, they agreed they could think of ways to cut back on household spending. Sixty-eight percent, for instance, indicated they could save by eating out less often. But only 18 percent indicated they were likely to do so.[40] Peterson wants to rescue an old word—"thrift." Instead of pinched austerity, he says, it should remind us of its root in the verb "to thrive"; indeed, for environmentalists it's a friendly word, implying a commitment to care and conservation. Be thrifty with money, with water, with energy. And it's the direction that many nations around the world seem slowly to be muddling toward.[41]

Even so, it's unlikely these governments will be able to sustain pensions and benefits of the size they've promised, and it's unclear they really should. When Social Security was launched, during the Depression, the program's Advisory Council (back in the days when bureaucrats could still write

English) insisted that "the pattern cannot be larger than the cloth." FDR said, "This act does not offer anyone an easy life," but merely "the minimum necessary to keep a foothold."[42] By 1996, however, the American elderly had a median per capita income 67 percent above that of the population as a whole; the average seventy-year-old spent 20 percent more each year than the average thirty-year-old; his net worth was $222,000, versus $66,000 for the typical forty-year-old.[43] Since Social Security pays out to everyone, regardless of how much they have, young low-income workers are essentially subsidizing upper-income elderly—if you work at Burger King, you're helping someone pay that note on the Winnebago with the I'M SPENDING MY KIDS' INHERITANCE sticker on the bumper. And they're not just "getting back what they paid in"—a couple who retired in 1960 got back eleven times their contribution, even after accounting for inflation and interest. By the 1980s, retirees were still getting back four times their contribution.[44] Even though the benefit formulas are supposed to be slightly progressive (the poorer elderly get a little more than their "share"), studies in the Netherlands, Sweden, Britain, and the United States found that there was no real redistribution of wealth—largely because rich people live (and hence collect) longer than poor people.[45] The system is, in other words, a disgrace.

It's a disgrace because there *are* in fact plenty of poorer old folk. Despite the high average incomes of the elderly, Social Security accounts for more than half the total income of retirees making less than $20,000 a year, and these people in turn comprise about half of all recipients.[46] It's these people—visit any trailer park in America—whose lives will be trashed if the system goes kaput. So why doesn't the government simply set a "means test" and figure out who actually needs Social Security? Because there's a bloc of committed voters who so far won't allow it. The American Association of Retired Persons, the nation's biggest lobby, insists that Social Security is an "entitlement"; furthermore, say many of their supporters, if it isn't a universal program, voters won't support it. In other words, if you don't subsidize a lot of Winnebagos, the Winnebago owners will make sure that no one subsidizes the people in the trailer parks. Employed by muscular young men on street corners, this argument would rightly be called a protection racket. And in a few places around the world progressives are rejecting it. A Labor government in Australia, for instance, decided in the 1980s not to abandon that nation's means test, on the grounds that "fair" didn't mean a handout to everyone. Instead, it decided that "the program is only fair if the pension is provided to those in actual need of it."[47]

• • •

So far, we've been talking less about *aging* than about *funding*—that's how politics defines the issue. It's far more interesting, though, simply to think about what it means to grow old at this point in history, about whether there are new ways we might want to live even if we weren't worried about Social Security.

Consider retirement, for instance. We get ready to retire at about sixty-five not because of some signal from our biological clock, but because of a signal from Otto von Bismarck, the nineteenth-century German prime minister. He wanted to give pensions to civil servants, but he didn't want to pay out very much, so his actuaries calculated that seventy would be a good choice; when there was protest, he backed down to sixty-five. Not that it made much difference—the average life expectancy in Germany was less than forty-five.[48] But though we live 60 percent longer than Bismarck's bureaucrats, he still rules our thinking about when to give up work; it's as if we still wore monocles because they were fashionable in his day. In fact, even as we live longer, we tend to retire earlier—the largest number of people now leave off work at sixty-two.[49] Even though most work is physically much easier than it used to be, only 16 percent of men work past the age of sixty-five.[50]

As a result, we live increasingly weird and unintegrated lives. In our earlier years we're time-starved; everyone wants more hours for themselves, for their family. People stay at the office half the night, and when they finally come in the door, they're blabbing away on the cellular. Polls show we'd even take salary cuts in exchange for a few more hours a week.[51] But when retirement comes, we have far more time than we know what to do with. Suddenly, there's twenty or thirty years stretching out ahead, and people must fill time, kill time, pass the time of day. When one group of California local government employees was asked if they'd like a scheme that would redistribute some of the leisure time now taken in retirement back into the middle years of their lives, more than 80 percent said yes.[52]

We keep, all of us, a mental calendar of our lives: we know when we're in our spring, we know when autumn approaches. But all of a sudden that calendar is out of whack. Summer lasts far longer than it used to; the fall is gentler. Plan your life by the old schedule and you'll put up storm windows on your life long before the first snow. Each year more and more vigorous people have no particular role in society; as Arlie Russell Hochschild points out in her study of the elderly, "status based on what one 'has done' is thinly based compared to status based on 'what one is doing.'"[53] One study after another demonstrates that older workers do just fine. When the Travelers Insurance Company started a job bank that allowed retired employees to return for forty hours a month of work, it found an enormous demand within the company for the retirees.[54] Computers don't daunt them; there are jobs available that allow older workers to thrive. The most serious barrier to part-time employment at good jobs for older workers, according to one study, is simply "the attitudes of the workers themselves and of their potential employers. . . . Many truly believe that productivity almost always declines with age, that 'old dogs cannot learn new tricks.'"[55] But that may be changing, at least among workers. One recent study showed that three-quarters of people over sixty-five said they'd like some kind of paying job.

What's important to remember, though, is that it's not just retiring at sixty-five that doesn't make much emotional sense; it's also working like a dog at forty-five when you need to be spending more time with your family. The physical fact of our longer lives should change our thinking, change it in significant ways. But so far it hasn't really sunk in. Perhaps it will eventually (baby boomers now tell pollsters that the value they most want to pass on to younger generations is "respect for the aged"),[56] but for the most part we still look on those years past sixty as a foreign country, as something separate from the rest of life. "You get a lot of handwringing about how expensive it's going to be to have a society where everyone's walking around with canes," says Lincoln Day, a demographer whose voice carries a bit of the reedy tremolo that comes with age. "But that turns out to be a small fraction of even the oldest people in society."[57] The same wave of medical technology that has increased life expectancy has also made old people healthier. A fractured hip no longer means sure disability. Cataracts are easy to eradicate. One Canadian study found that 95.4 percent of those between sixty-five and seventy-four were still living in their own households.[58] Disabilities among

American elderly have declined 15 percent since 1982, according to the National Academy of Sciences. "And not only are there fewer disabled people, those who are disabled seem to have fewer disabilities."[59] Only 15 percent of those over sixty-five are frail or sick—only 15 percent.[60]

This is vital information; if you don't know it in your bones, you'll make decisions about your life that don't make sense, decisions that made sense in nineteenth-century Germany. You can expect twenty or thirty more years of life, and those twenty or thirty years have been added not to the end but to the middle. "The period between what was formerly the end of middle age (roughly fifty) and what is now the beginning of real, physical old age (some point after seventy-five) is a new stage in adult life," writes Lydia Bronte. It implies all sorts of changes, for institutions even more important than pensions. Exiting school when you're twenty-two may have made sense when you only had another twenty-two years to live, for instance, but when you're likely still to be hard at work half a century later, we need new models, new notions.

•   •   •

Part of our reluctance to change our thinking about age comes from our sense that an older society is less dynamic, less creative. "We're afraid that as we get an older society, we will lose our innovative capacity, our adaptability to a changing world," says Makoto Atoh, director-general of the Japanese government's Institute of Population Problems. As Nicholas Kristof put it in *The New York Times*, "Would Bill Gates have founded Microsoft if he had been a septuagenarian? Would he even have used Windows?"[61]

It's an old idea, of course, but in its scientific incarnation it dates from about 1905, when the great medico Sir William Osler gave his farewell address from Johns Hopkins University (the same institution where G. Stanley Hall first won fame, and about the same time). In his lecture, entitled "The Fixed Period," Osler expounded his view on "the comparative uselessness of men above forty years of age" and the complete uselessness of men above the age of sixty, referring his listeners to a novel of Trollope's in which "the plot hinges on the admirable scheme of a college into which at sixty men retired for a year of contemplation before a peaceful departure by chloroform." Osler failed to take his own advice, filling a professorship at Oxford until he was seventy, but his views attracted many followers. Robert Woodworth, in his widely used early textbook *Psychology: A Study of Mental Life*, put the case this way:

Seldom does a very old person get outside the limits of his previous habits. Few great inventions, artistic or practical, have emanated from really old persons, and comparatively few even from the middle-aged. . . . The period from twenty years up to forty seems to be the most favorable for inventiveness.

A University of Ohio psychologist, Harvey Lehman, set out to see if Woodworth was right. For twenty years he carefully tabulated and cross-checked, until in 1953 he published *Age and Achievement*, which indeed seemed to show that in chemistry, in medicine, in philosophy, music, art, and literature, men hit their peaks between thirty and forty. He was soon rebutted by other researchers, though, who demonstrated that his data didn't take into account shorter life spans. In eras when most people died by forty, it stood to reason that their great work would be done by then. Who knows what an elderly Shelley might have written?

Meanwhile, new brain research began to show interesting things. Though the total weight of a brain declined roughly 11 percent from early adulthood to age eighty, the neurons of an eighty-year-old brain show far more *interconnections* than those of a normal fifty-year-old. In any event, a century in which people began to regularly live longer lives started to prove Osler wrong; Toscanini, Casals, Picasso—the list is by now extensive.[62] If Picasso had died at forty, he would have proved the old point; that he died past ninety, still painting masterpieces, undermines it.

I wrote earlier that my father, after a life as a newspaperman, recently wrote his first book. To see the ease with which he reported and organized huge masses of material, and the suppleness with which he wrote, changed my own thinking. He'd mastered a difficult new skill; it made me reconsider my father, which is a hard thing to do.

Observing those around us, observing our own lives, we tend to see aging differently from the stereotypes. When Louis Harris surveyed elderly Americans, he found that while 40 percent believed ill health afflicted old people in general, only 21 percent had been sick themselves. Forty-five percent were sure that loneliness troubled senior citizens generally, but only 13 percent reported being lonely themselves.[63] We assume older people are more conservative, but before *Roe v. Wade* in 1973, polls showed more older women supporting legal abortions than young ones; among congressmen, hawks and doves on the issue of the war in Vietnam had the same median age. Probably the most elderly society on earth is Sweden's, and it may be the most progressive as well.[64]

All of which is to say that "old people" are endlessly more variable than we've thought; why, they're almost like real human beings. And that in essence there are far fewer "old people" than the demographic charts would lead us to expect. Demographer Lincoln Day suggests that instead of calling people old based on the number of their birthdays, we might calculate the number whose life expectancy is ten years or less. By that reckoning, even if the population of Britain someday falls to what it was on the eve of World War II, only 16.7 percent of Britons will be aged, compared with 23.1 percent if you were simply counting everyone above sixty-five.[65] There's still aging going on—we are, in fact, all of us quite likely to die—but it's not alarming in quite the ways we're used to thinking about.

You can go overboard with all of this rethinking. In her book *New Passages*, a chipper Gail Sheehy wrote about fifty-five-year-old women having egg-donor babies, about seventy-year-old men reversing aging by twenty years with growth hormones, and she compared it to the opening of the American West. "At the dawn of a new century it is the adult life cycle itself—stretching it, taming it, bringing it under control, making it yield its riches—that beckons us all, women and men alike. This is the new human frontier."[66] She looks forward to the Serene Sixties, the Sage Seventies, the Uninhibited Eighties, the Nobility of the Nineties, the Celebratory Centenarians; as Alan Wolfe points out in a perceptive review in *The New Republic*, "a younger generation wanting to renounce its obligations to its parents could devise no better strategy than to picture them as leading lives of bliss."[67] Every old person will at some point need to lean on others, and on society as a whole; by the same token, though, to insist on treating people as feeble because of the number of their birthdays makes no more sense than to keep children in school until they're thirty. At every age we need some independence and some dependence; the luckiest lives have the best ratios.

What I'm trying to say is this: we approach the "problem" of "aging" by carefully keeping our thinking inside a box, a box constructed by Otto von Bismarck. According to his plan, the "solution" to old age is that everyone cease work on or around his sixty-fifth birthday and start getting a government check, needed or not. We will distort our economies and our politics trying to keep his particular vision alive; worse, we will distort our lives. And perhaps worse still, we will miss a huge chance as a society to change some of our basic institutions in ways that would not only make life easier for a larger elderly population but also help with our environmental troubles.

• • •

I remember with great affection my wife's grandmother, Esther Rogoff, a child of the Lower East Side who grew up to help her husband run a small pickle factory in the Bronx and then, after his death, moved to Yonkers. She lived there in an apartment building with a few women from her old neighborhood, and she soon made friends with many other tenants. She led a useful life—charity work, keeping far-flung relatives in touch with each other, reading. The only drawback to her existence was Central Avenue, the four-lane boulevard that ran directly in front of her apartment building, separating it from the strip shopping mall on the other side. She didn't trust herself to cross it on foot, and with good reason—it was made for cars; the few crosswalks had short lights. And even if she'd made it across, six or seven acres of parking separated her from the stores. So she depended on her family to drive once a week or so from a nearby suburb and take her shopping. That was fine—it's what family is for. But her life would have been a little richer if she could have made that trip herself, any day the weather was good.

What slows down as people age? Not minds, necessarily. But reflexes, muscles. Which means that thinking about the *how* of living becomes more important. "Something that might seem a superficial matter, a mere question of where one lives, can in some cases have a surprisingly deep effect on the shape and feel of the old person's social world," writes Arlie Russell Hochschild.[68] Often that means something as simple as being able to cross the street. In Canberra, Australia, 613 older residents were surveyed; the report found many things, but one of the most specific, as reported by the *Canberra Times*, "is that the green 'walk' period at intersections should be longer because it seems to cater for young things who will gambol across the road rather than for the aging who may take longer and who at the moment are often forced to scuttle to make it."[69]

The Canberra study was actually a comparison with the Hague, in the Netherlands. The Dutch city features "a pattern of residence characterized by high-density townhouses with small private gardens, where there is ready access to public parks, shops, and a wide range of services, and where the main means of getting to distant friends, volunteer work, the beach, the doctor, the occasional film is to cycle, bus, or walk." The Australian city, by contrast, sprawled on the American model, "where public parks or shops tend to be some distance from one's place of residence, where neighborhoods are separated from one another by large heavily trafficked roads, and where the main means of getting to places, for want of any suitable alternatives, is the private automobile."[70] A soccer mom with a station wagon can manage either layout, but for a soccer mom's mom, the Hague would be infinitely preferable.

Which is why the baby boom generation, as it ages, has the chance to finally change America in remarkable ways—to change its very shape. Always before, the self-interest of the boomers has been at odds with their oft-professed concern for the world: the environment may have mattered to them, but not, on the whole, as much as making a pile of money. As they age, however, the generation that launched Earth Day can make a difference *every* day. With enough will, you can change your surroundings pretty fast; consider Curitiba, a city of several million in the south of Brazil, where the local government built the world's best bus system from scratch in two decades. It's a wonderful place not to own a car—old and young walk and ride the bus *everywhere*. And as a result residents of the city use 25 percent less fuel than other Brazilians.[71] Twenty-five percent is a big number, big enough to begin to address some of the problems like global warming now threatening us. And it didn't even take that much money, just a certain amount of imagination translated into political will.

It's the next generation of elderly people that will decide the question, that will either accomplish these changes or cling barnaclelike to Bismarck's crabbed vision. As Lester Thurow points out, "long before they are a technical majority of the population, the elderly will be unstoppable politically, since those under 18 can't vote and those between 18 and 30 tend not to."[72] At the moment, that political muscle is mainly used to protest any cuts in Social Security—the reform commission headed by Senators Robert Kerrey and John Danforth, for instance, received 350,000 outraged postcards from seniors before it had even considered any recommendations.[73] Except for the Catholic Church, the AARP is the largest organization in America; its *Bulletin* has more subscribers than *Reader's Digest* or *TV Guide*.[74] All that power could build new bus lines, rezone suburbs, accomplish all the mundane but mammoth tasks that would reshape the country, or it could freeze the status quo.

In a sense, then, what we face is the test of a simple proposition: does age bring with it maturity? Let's define maturity this way: as the understanding that you're not at the center of creation, the most important thing in the world. It's hard for anyone succored by a consumer culture to mature—we've been told too often to "Have It Your Way." But it's maturity we need, maturity that must undergird any sustainable world. Only mature people might utter the two words our civilization most desperately needs to hear: "That's enough." And it's mature men and women we still admire most, even in a world that's superficially devoted to Choices, to Options, to Plastic Surgery. If Modern Maturity, to borrow the name of the AARP magazine, is going to be about screwing the grandkids to guarantee every red cent of the pension Otto von Bismarck promised you, then the boomers will die as they lived: big talkers. But age is supposed to bring a certain kind of wisdom, the understanding that past a certain point material things can't satisfy us in the deepest ways. If the next generation of elderly can summon the maturity to invest much of their money in things that will make their own lives easier and also ease some of the planet's strains, then they will finally have realized the great ambition of their youth and turned the world upside down.

It's not such a long distance from talking about having a single child to talking about making the country elder-friendly. Not only are they linked by demography, they're also connected by the realization that we could, if we decided to do so, change what seems inevitable. We don't need to expand our population 50 percent; we don't need to grow old scuttling across intersections. We can make choices.

chapter

seven

CHISELED ABOVE THE HUGE FRONT DOORS OF MANHATTAN'S CENTRAL POST OFFICE, YOU WILL FIND THE FOLLOWING INscription: NEITHER SNOW NOR RAIN NOR HEAT NOR GLOOM OF NIGHT STAYS THESE COURIERS FROM THE SWIFT COMPLETION OF THEIR APPOINTED ROUNDS. The words are from Herodotus, and they're carved in stone across the 280-foot entrance because— the building's architect thought they sounded stirring. It's the only place they appear; it's not the motto of the Postal Service, much less a guarantee.[1] The words represent, perhaps, an aspiration.

A few miles away, off lower Manhattan, you'll find Emma Lazarus's famous poem ("Give me your tired, your poor, your huddled masses yearning to breathe free") on the Statue of Liberty. Or, actually, not *on* the statue. It's inside the pedestal, engraved on a small plaque that a friend of hers placed there twenty years after the statue was dedicated. It's not a motto either, nor a guarantee. The real name of the statue is *Liberty Enlightening the World*, and its French sculptor, Frédéric Auguste Bartholdi, wrote of his work, "I will try especially to glorify the Republic and Liberty over there, *hoping that I will one day find them back here.*"[2]

Which is a way of saying that the issue of immigration has become encrusted with as many layers of myth and emotion as, say, the issue of only children. I'm in favor—reluctantly, painfully—of moderate reductions in the number of immigrants coming into this country. But to explain why (and also why I reject the calls of some environmentalists for more draconian cuts) will take a little reflection, a little calm. Because even if Lazarus's poem is not national doctrine, it has become one of our symbols of nationhood, and of a profoundly decent aspiration—to be a welcoming civilization and a refuge.

Save for those who were here originally and those brought here by force, virtually all of us are children or grandchildren or great-great-great-grandchildren of that aspiration. What's more, we have become a rich country in a poor world. It is therefore no wonder that immigration is hard for us to talk about, even harder than aging. A large part of me does not want even to address this topic, and I suppose I could dodge it since it diverges in some ways from my main point—the possibility of smaller families. But there is no honest way to avoid it, because immigrants account for much of our population growth.

Exactly how much is hard to say. If you read the fundraising pamphlets from groups like FAIR (the Federation for American Immigration Reform), for instance, you are left with the clear idea we are being overrun:

Immigration now adds more than one million people—the equivalent of two Washington D.C.'s—to our population each year. At our current pace of immigration, our population will grow to 400 million people by 2050.[3]

But a million a year won't get us anywhere near 400 million by 2050; we're also having lots of babies. The Census Bureau, in its "middle series" of population estimates, says that by 2050 the population may include 82 million post-1992 immigrants and their descendants, about half the total population growth in that period. And some statisticians say even that calculation is too high. Robert Warren, director of the Statistics Division of the U.S. Immigration and Naturalization Service, recently calculated that "if immigration were expressed as a proportion of gross *addition* to the population, then fertility adds four times as much to the population as immigration."[4] In other words, it's complicated.

Clearly, though, immigration adds many bodies to the roster of Americans each year. And not only is it substantial, but for people interested in quickly controlling the growth of our population, it offers one other seeming advantage: the government, thank God, can't control your reproduction, but if Congress passed a law, it would turn off the immigration spigot, at least for those who arrive legally.

So it is no wonder that discussions of immigration usually turn ugly right away, that almost everyone with any sense shies away from the issue—it's as toxic as abortion, as radioactive as the Middle East. Much safer to stick with recycling. Consider what happened last fall with the Sierra Club. A Cleveland engineer, Alan Kuper, managed to get 2,000 other club members to support his call for a referendum question that would put the club on record in favor of limiting immigration for environmental reasons. But before the members could even vote, the club's board of directors reported that it had been "besieged" with calls opposing the policy, and overwhelmingly rejected the proposal. One board member said, "Immigration is a political issue, and not an environmental issue." Another club member insisted that "the immigrants are not the polluters. They come here and use public transportation."[5] This country's record on race is so hideous that such discussions founder almost before they begin. "To us it seems like immigrant-bashing that's trying to dress up in green," says Frank Sharry, executive director of the National Immigration Forum.[6] "This is such a messy issue for environmentalists," says Roy Beck, a journalist who has written books about the topic. "We like to feel good about what we do, and immigration is so full of political negatives."[7]

And yet none of that has stopped some environmental groups, usually those on the fringes of the movement, from making immigration a central issue—perhaps the central issue—in their efforts to protect the nation. Consider, for instance, the Carrying Capacity Network, a Washington-based advocacy group, which last year published a huge two-volume compendium of articles and studies about why we need smaller populations. Most of it was useful—articles about dwindling energy supplies, soil erosion, grain yields. But they also reprinted articles asserting that "the Balkans charnel house is a paradigm realization of multiculturalism,"[8] or scolding Mexican aliens for waving a Mexican flag during a California rally.[9] One of the group's board members, writing under a pseudonym, even proposed a system of computerized National Identity Cards (NICs), which citizens would need to open their front doors, start their cars, or get a job. People "who depend on criminal or useless activity for a livelihood" may protest, "but honest citizens will very much prefer life in a NIC-based society. They will realize that NICs make life hard for criminals and social parasites, and easy and pleasant for honest and productive citizens."[10]

Such extremism has roots within the radical wings of the environmental movement. Ecologist Garrett Hardin wrote a famous essay in the 1970s enunciating what he called a "lifeboat ethics." He likened our nation to a small dinghy surrounded by a hundred drowning swimmers, and counseled admitting "no more to the boat" to increase its chances of not being swamped by environmental cataclysm. To those who say "I feel guilty about my good luck," he offered a simple reply: "Get out and yield your place to others."[11] Others have refined and amplified his argument; Virginia Abernethy, the editor of the journal *Population and Environment*, says easy immigration makes the whole world into a "commons" where no one has any incentive to conserve; she cites statistics to show that the mere possibility of emigrating to the U.S. raises birthrates in other nations. "A relatively closed U.S. border would create most vividly an image of limits and be an incentive to restrict family size," she insists.[12] Somewhat more vividly, Edward Abbey, the great (and cantankerous) desert novelist and essayist, recommended stopping immigration cold: "Yes, I know, if the American Indians had enforced such a policy none of us pale-faced honkies would be here. But the Indians were foolish, and divided, and failed to keep our WASP ancestors out. They've regretted it ever since."[13] The argument of all these opponents is quite explicit: forget the Christian ethic about being your brother's keeper; forget the moral qualms that come from shutting the door on desperately poor people. In the long run, it's better for all concerned if we're stern.

The trouble is, though, we keep feeling guilty. And with good reason, I'm afraid. Lifeboat ethics don't work so well when you're sailing on a yacht. We could still take in some of those drowning passengers if we were willing to throw a bit of our *stuff* overboard, and in our heart of hearts we know that.

To understand why we will never ban immigration outright, and why we never should, pick up *The New York Times* for January 9, 1997. On the front page, you'll find the story about a twenty-eight-year-old Indian woman who each day must decide whether to buy food for her children or buy kerosene to boil the water they drink. She has too few rupees to do both, so she usually serves them unboiled water—even though it has already killed two of her children. The reporter, Nicholas Kristof, notes that 2.9 billion humans lack proper sanitation. *That's half the people on this planet.* "All in all," he writes, "human wastes may be more menacing than nuclear waste, for feces kill far more people than radioactive substances."[14]

But it's not simply a sense of justice that causes many to support immigration. A little deeper into the same day's paper, in the Metro section, Celia W. Dugger reports about the recent surge of immigrants to New York City—560,000 from 1990 to 1994, "transforming its neighborhoods, filling its schools and staffing its small businesses." Mayor Rudolph Giuliani, speaking at Ellis Island, said: "For those people in New York who are concerned—'Oh, there are too many foreigners coming here and there are too many people that look different or act different'—please remember that has been the key to our success."[15]

Meanwhile, on the entertainment page, Ralph Blumenthal explains that an audience of foreign tourists is now crucial to Broadway's success: "English is almost a second language at

'Cats,'" says a spokesman for the musical.[16] And on the front page of the business section, Glenn Collins writes from Pillsbury headquarters in Minneapolis that the company has become "the world's biggest maker of Mexican fare," employing an electron microscope to study "the porosity of tortilla shells."[17]

That's just one day's paper, picked nearly at random; it shows to me how routine the flow of people and ideas back and forth across borders has become. No one's more than a plane ticket away, and by now everyone's seen what it looks like here. A billion people a week watch *Baywatch*. In that kind of world, simply cutting off immigration is both a moral and political impossibility.

And yet the other vision can be just as extreme. In his farewell address to the nation, Ronald Reagan described his America as a shining city on the hill where "if there had to be walls, the walls had doors and the doors were open to anyone with the will and heart to get there."[18] Open to anyone? Is our moral duty that broad, or nearly that broad? Even if the population of California, currently 30 million, is expected to reach 50 million in just fifty years?[19] Is it our moral duty forever?

In hard fact, it's clear that no more than a tiny minority—one-half of 1 percent, maybe—of the world's poor people will ever get to live in the United States, even if we double our immigration levels, even if we decide our borders could contain half a billion people. Almost all the masses will still be huddled. Very few of the immigrants we do admit are refugees—only about 10 percent, a tiny dent in the list of 40 million or so displaced people around the world. And the money spent admitting and resettling one refugee here would maintain five hundred abroad.[20] It's not a black-and-white issue, and it's not entirely a brown-and-white one either; some studies show almost as much support among recent Mexican-born newcomers as among Anglos for limiting immigrants.[21]

So maybe it's better to stay with the physical, the pragmatic. I've explained at great length already why I think the facts of atmospheric chemistry, the risks of dramatic changes in the planet's physical system, argue for trying to stabilize the number of people living in this super-consuming nation. You could do that by eliminating immigration entirely; you could do it by allowing immigration to continue as at present and reducing the fertility rate below one child per couple, a level never seen on the planet; or you could do it by some combination.

There is no obvious way to arrive at a precise right number for either fertility or immigration; the best you can do is triangulate from what seems possible, feasible, somewhat fair. A fertility level of 1.5 children per woman—that's as many families with one child as with two, and a certain number with lots, and a certain number with none—seems possible. It's lower than we've ever seen in this country, but it's slightly higher than in Italy and Spain, which have the lowest birthrates on earth. It's where Japan is right now.[22]

And if you simultaneously limited legal immigration to 400,000, about half its current level, then in 2050 we'd have about 230 million Americans—about the same number we did in 1983.

There's nothing magic about 400,000 immigrants. It's not the "right" number. But it's not entirely picked from thin air, either; it's a little below the annual average of immigrants during the Great Wave of 1880–1924, and double the annual average of the years from 1925 to 1965. It's the number suggested by a commission headed by Nelson Rockefeller in 1972, and 50,000 above the number suggested by a 1981 commission headed by Father Theodore Hesburgh.[23] It's the number that were immigrating to this country in the early 1970s when polls showed most Americans saying, for the first time in decades, that perhaps the level of new arrivals was high enough. It won't satisfy those who want a moratorium, or a token 100,000 a year; it won't satisfy Ronald Reagan. And I make no claim that it's *fair*—immigrant 400,001 will be just as desperate, just as deserving, as immigrant 399,999.

In fact, it's unforgivably harsh. In a world where 2.9 billion people have no toilet, who are any of us to say "Go away" simply because we had the luck to be born in an easy place. It will condemn many people to a harder, poorer life; if it didn't, immigration levels would scarcely matter, since living like an American in Mexico or the Philippines would do just as much damage to the atmosphere.

It's so harsh that I think there's little chance we'd stick to anything like it unless we'd also decided to make certain changes ourselves—decided, one by one, that we might have smaller families ourselves, for instance. At the moment, we're not hard on immigration—even if we sense that the country at the start of the twenty-first century is full—in part because we know we're not hard on ourselves. Unwilling to make even marginal gestures toward the future ourselves—to save money, to conserve, to consume less, to pay more taxes—how can we deny other people the *total* change of future that immigration represents?

And yet the facts of our environmental predicament are hard ones. If we face them squarely, if among other things we start consuming less and having fewer children, then we earn some right to tell the truth to others, too, however painful that truth might be. This *is* a moral question, but it's also a math problem.

• • •

It's worth noting what will happen here if we *don't* lower our birthrates and reduce immigration. Our population will rise from its current 260 million to as many as 400 million by the middle of the century: a child born today could share this nation with 50 percent more people before she reaches middle age. Fifty percent is a lot.

We don't talk about this much. One researcher studied the stories journalists wrote in recent years about urban sprawl, water shortages, and endangered species. Of the thousands of articles he dredged up, only one in ten mentions population growth as a source of the problem, and only one in a hundred mentions population stability as a possible solution.[24] When writing about water in California, say, a newspaper reporter might discuss drought and she might discuss irrigation, but she will rarely if ever discuss the sheer difficulty of trying to supply the 30 million who live there now, never mind the 50 million who will be there soon.[25] "It's such an incendiary issue," explained one reporter. "If you say 'It all comes down to too many people,' you'll have everybody from Operation Rescue to the Catholic Church calling you."[26]

Of course, as we've seen, it *doesn't* all come down to population (our appetites and our technologies count just as much); and as we shall see later, the obstacles to change lie less with clerics than we think. But the point is clear: it's a question we remain afraid to discuss here at home. When we think about Africa, we think about population. But here at home less than half of Americans surveyed in 1993 agreed that lowering the U.S. birthrate was important for the environment.[27]

Partly this nonchalance must stem from our long sense that America could handle—indeed required—more people. Ben

Franklin, in a letter to a London friend during the early months of the Revolution, noted triumphantly that Britain "at the expense of three million pounds has killed one hundred and fifty Yankees this campaign. . . . During the same time, sixty thousand children have been born in America."[28] A few years later Hector St. John de Crèvecoeur put it plainly in his widely read letters back to Europe: "There is room for every body in America. . . . Instead of starving, he will be fed; instead of being idle, he will have employment; and these are riches enough for such men as come over here."[29] There are some who think that way still; jetting over the desert of the Southwest, or the northern Plains, they imagine that this is still an empty country, though for reasons I outlined in Part 2, this is a delusion.

Others fall victim to another misconception—that most population growth in this country comes from an "epidemic" of "teenage mothers." It's true that our teenage birthrate is the highest in the industrialized world—sixteen times higher than Japan's[30] and on a par with Haiti's.[31] And it's true that those children have more problems, and are more likely to be neglected. As Alan Durning and Christopher Crowther point out in a recent report called *Misplaced Blame*, childhood poverty, sexual abuse, and inadequate family planning all spur growth.[32] The poor mountain counties of New York, where I live, are much like the backwoods they describe in the Pacific Northwest, where high school graduation often features a new mother or two. It's absurd that federal support for family planning services has dropped almost 70 percent since 1980.[33]

And yet these are not the only causes for population growth. Birthrates among adolescent girls have been constant since 1950 relative to the total birthrate; the great majority of these births are to 18- and 19-year-old women, not to "babies having babies"; two-thirds of teenage parents are white, non-

Hispanic, and nonpoor;[34] and most births outside of marriage are to women in their twenties and thirties.[35] Contrary to common belief, black birthrates are now near the national average, and black teenage birthrates have declined 20 percent since 1991.[36] Undoubtedly, if we were willing to educate our kids about sex as diligently as our media educates them about sexiness, we could reduce teenage births dramatically (American kids are no more likely to have sex than kids in France, England, Canada, or Holland, but two to seven times likelier to become pregnant).[37] Even if we did so, though, our population would continue to grow. If the birthrate of women who have not finished high school fell to the level of those who have, it would reduce the annual number of births by just 3 percent.[38] By 1993, 40 percent of women having a third child in their forties were college graduates, double the rate of only a decade before. Those couples often "view it as a sign of prosperity to have more children and be able to support them well," one psychologist told *The Wall Street Journal*. In the words of a forty-six-year-old mother, "It's obliterating middle age for me. When I walked into my high school reunion, everybody shrieked because I was pregnant."[39]

The final misconception about our population is that it is growing "slowly"—which it is, when compared to Zambia or Peru. But 1 percent annually, our present rate,[40] adds up fast; at that pace we would be nearing 1 billion Americans before the next century is out. If we grew at our historical pace for the next two hundred years, we'd have 15 billion Americans by 2200.[41] But let's don't think that far ahead—long-term forecasts are pretty useless. Let's stick with the next few decades. Four hundred million Americans by 2050—that's the "middle series" estimate of the Census Bureau. What would that *feel* like?

•   •   •

The first thing it would feel like is more crowded. We don't
live spread out across the Plains, because the Plains are not
hospitable country for large numbers of people. We jam ourselves in along the coasts—more so all the time. Fifty percent
of Americans live on 10 percent of the continental land mass
along the coasts. By 1990, the coastal region of the Northeast
had a population density of 767 people per square mile, 100
more than El Salvador, the most densely populated country
in the hemisphere.[42] And as we pack ourselves into those
places, we change them; an area of 1.3 million acres, an area
the size of Delaware, is covered by pavement each year.[43] If
we continue sprawling at the same pace as we have since
1977, by 2050 the urbanized area of the United States will
have doubled to 312,000 square miles, an area larger than
Wisconsin, Iowa, Illinois, Indiana, Ohio, and Michigan combined.[44] We *could* live somewhat more compactly, we *could*
tame some of that sprawl, but at the moment the *average*
Americans are building ever-bigger houses. It's a reasonable
bet to conclude that 50 percent more people would mean
nearly 50 percent more houses, driveways, cars. Across most
of the nation, a third or more of new development between
1982 and 1992 took place on "prime farmland." In California's Central Valley alone, where population is expected to
triple by 2040, a million acres of farmland may be lost for
good.[45] If you want a rule of thumb, says Cornell's David Pimentel, at the moment each person added to our population
requires devoting one acre of land to urbanization and road
building.

All of which sounds kind of abstract. So look at a particular place that most Americans have visited: Florida. By 2020,
Florida's population of 14 million people will rise to at least 20

million, and by some estimates as much as 27 million. The state lost 2 million acres of farmland to development between 1982 and 1992 alone; by one calculation, the coming growth will require as many as 168,000 miles of new roads. "The increase in congestion in the last ten years has been phenomenal," says a University of South Florida traffic expert. "The increase in the next ten years will be *astronomical.*"[46] You can't prevent Florida from overcrowding simply by reducing fertility and immigration; you'd also have to do something about all that sun, all those beaches, that keep drawing people from other parts of America. But it does give a sense of what life might be like as our population continues to climb toward 400 million.

Americans who love wild places already have some sense of that crowding. You can find lonely and never-visited spots, plenty of them, but you can also find crowds at every national park and state campground. Some regard this as a sentimental, or a selfish, thing to worry over, and yet it seems to me crucial. We can live without big wilderness, but it's not clear we can live as *Americans,* not in the way we have in the past. Wallace Stegner, the mighty western writer, put it this way:

> Many Americans—a majority if we believe the polls—have it in their *blood* to be members and advocates of untrammeled nature. They don't need consequences to teach them. For while we were working so ruthlessly on the wilderness, it was working on us. It altered our habits, our cuisine, our language, our expectations, our images, our heroes. It put a curve in our axe helves and a bend in our religion. It built something into our national memory. . . . Many people who never or rarely get to enjoy wild nature have a belief in its rightness.

He describes his granddaughter on an Outward Bound trip to Death Valley, where she spent three days alone up on a slope of the Panamints. "I know that before it was over it was the greatest experience of her young life. She may have greater ones later on, but she will never quite get over this one. . . . And if millions of Americans have not been so lucky as she, why, all the more reason to save intact some of the places to which those who are moved to do so may go, and grow by it."[47] In the words of the Kentucky farmer-essayist Wendell Berry, "We are a remnant people in a remnant country. We have come, or are coming fast, to the end of what we were given."[48]

I'm not quite as despairing as that. I live in the mountains of the East, which have recovered in wondrous ways from the cutting and pasturing that denuded them a century ago. The Adirondacks are more wild now than they were two, three, four, and five generations ago. That morning in Griffin, as I was leaving John Teachout's house, I came across a big she-bear. She stood her ground longer than I expected before she waddled into the woods—this was her place far more than it was mine. But even the Adirondacks—even the northern Rockies, even Alaska—will be less wild a generation hence if our population and its effects keep growing. Every year brings another thousand homes to the Adirondacks, most of them summer places for those people crowding the eastern coasts; every year sees a few more lakes succumb to acid rain; every year the higher temperatures stress the forest a little more. Wildness doesn't disappear in a day. It erodes so slowly that you don't notice it going. But it does go.

Much the same could be said about democracy, about our political life. I grew up in Lexington, Massachusetts, the "birthplace of American liberty," and spent my summers wearing a tricorne hat and giving tours of the Battle Green, where Americans first fought for the idea that we should control our own destinies. And so my natural drift is toward a radical democracy, exemplified by the town meeting. But past a certain size, that becomes impossible. For many years even Lexington has had a "representative" town meeting, with elected delegates from each precinct, not the pure participation that comes with everyone crowding into the town hall on a March evening. When the United States was founded, each congressman took care of 30,000 voters. Now he or she has 570,000 constituents, a twentyfold dilution.[49] When we are 400 million, each "representative" will represent a million of us. It's *possible* to imagine democracy working well with those kinds of numbers, just as it's *possible* to imagine compact and clustered housing developments. It's *easier* to imagine a worsening rule by special interests. This country's democracy has often been called an experiment. And, as in a laboratory, we are now stressing it, stretching it to see how far it can go before it breaks.

There is, so far as I have been able to figure out, no way to reckon the perfect population for the United States or anywhere else, though many people have tried. Paul Ehrlich and his wife Anne wrote that "if we were forced to make an estimate of the optimum population size of the United States, we'd guess around 75 million," the population at the turn of the last century when the United States had both big cities and big wilderness. "At about that number we believe a permanently sustainable nation with a high quality of life could be designed."[50] David Pimentel, at Cornell, has made two different estimates of a sustainable population. The first time his computer said our nation could support between 40 million and 100 million; a few years later, when he changed some of his assumptions about solar energy, he estimated 200 million.

In fact, though, the number depends too much on how we live, on what we value. You can list constraints—we are losing topsoil eighteen times faster than we are replacing it; we are drawing groundwater 25 percent faster than it is being replenished[51]—but at some level the statistics mean little. It's as much a question of *feel*, of sensing the strains on the land and the society that come with bigness. I think we're getting signals now—from the temperature, from the wind, from the rising sea, from the strip malls spreading a half-mile farther each year—that we're big enough. That it's time to back off a little.

And since I live in a place where people have backed off some, I know that it's possible, that it's not synonymous with decline and deterioration and decay. From the window where I write, I can see the remains of a seventy-five-year-old sawmill, where the man who built my house once spent his days cutting boards. It was a good living, and by every account he was a good man whose memory still lingers; to my oldest neighbors I still live in the Charlie Kenyon place.

But the sawmill's been gone for several generations. The forest has come rushing back in with the exuberance that lots of rain and snow allows, and behind the forest have come the bears and bobcats. And now we're talking about the wolf coming back, too. Seventy-five years ago that would not have been possible; it was too crowded here, too dense with small subsistence farms. It's not that the farms were wrong and the wolf right, nor the other way around. It's that there are all sorts of sweet things in this world, many of which are us, and many of which are not.

Getting smaller, taking a step back—those notions have their own quiet glory.

PART FOUR

SELF

chapter

eight

THE BUILDING WAS NONDESCRIPT: FOUR STORIES OF MODERN CONCRETE JUST DOWN THE STREET FROM OTTAWA'S CIVIC HOSpital. The receptionist greeted me politely, told me the doctor was running a little late. And so I sat on the couch next to the old and dog-eared magazines, and read one more time the list of questions Dr. Phil McGuire wanted his vasectomy patients to answer before he performed the Procedure:

What would you and your partner feel if you were told tomorrow that she was pregnant? Joy? Despair? Resignation? What about in five years?

Would you want the chance to have children with another partner, if your current relationship ended through separation or death?

Would you want to have the chance to have more children if one or more of your children died?

> Would more children be in your picture now if your financial circumstances improved significantly?

These are tougher questions than you usually get asked in a doctor's office. If you have heart disease, you have to choose *what* to do; it's rare to have to choose, until the very end, whether you want to do *anything at all*. But I could have gotten up and left, no harm done.

Then Dr. McGuire came in, wearing khakis, old Nikes, an earring, a plaid shirt. So far that day, he said, he'd done nine vasectomies, pruned branches of nine family trees. He was calm, gentle—sweet. "I had a couple this morning who'd had one child when they were in their thirties, spent the next ten years trying to have another, and failed. Now they are in their early forties and just couldn't conceive of conceiving again, so they wanted some insurance." He'd had a police officer, and a guy who builds Web pages, and several couples in their early thirties, each with two kids.

And he'd talked with all of them. "I try to protect people if I don't think they're ready," he said. "I'm a general practitioner and I've seen so many women come in who are unexpectedly pregnant, and completely delighted about it." But when people have made up their minds, he's ready to help. He's done 1,100 vasectomies, more and more each year. "Someday I hope to have a clinic just devoted to vasectomies—a fish tank and all the hunting and fishing and outdoors magazines," he said. I'd come to him because Ottawa is not far from my home in upstate New York, because I could afford him (he charged just over $200, less than the cost of most American operations), and because I could tell from his Web site (www.ottawa-vas.com) that he thought pretty deeply about the whole issue. He had a sense of humor (his toll-free number is 1-800-LAST-KID), but he also had a sense of purpose. "Sometimes I turn people down," he said. "But it's so much safer than having a woman get a tubal ligation, which is a big operation inside a major body cavity with general anesthesia."

So I sat on the table, and pulled my pants down around my ankles, and he swabbed my scrotum with iodine ("the iodine needs to be a little warm—the last thing we want is any shrinkage before we start"), and then he injected a slug of anesthetic into each side of my testicles. Yes, it was a needle down there, but no, it didn't hurt much; by chance I'd spent the previous afternoon in the dentist's chair, and this was much less painful. (And no flossing!) He cut a small hole in my scrotum, and with a forceps pulled out the vas deferens, the tube that carried sperm to my penis. Then he cauterized it and put it back inside, repeating the procedure on the other side. I could feel a little tugging, nothing more. The wound was so small it didn't require stitches, or even a Band-Aid. For a few days, he said, my groin would be a little sore. After that it would take twenty ejaculations or so to drain the last of the sperm already in my system. And that would be that. In evolutionary terms, I'd be out of business.

•   •   •

It's easy for me to explain *why* I was lying on the table at the Ottawa Vasectomy Clinic: all I need is a string of statistics. In one recent study, condoms broke 4.8 percent of the time that they were used.[1] Sixty percent of all pregnancies in the U.S. are unintended—*sixty percent*.[2] That doesn't mean all those children are unwanted; half just come when their parents weren't planning on it, but half end in abortion.[3] In fact, six in ten women having abortions did so because their contraceptives failed; among typical couples, 18 percent using diaphragms and 12 percent using condoms managed to get pregnant. And no one's doing much to improve the situation: a nation that spends $600 million developing new cosmetics and fragrances each year has exactly one pharmaceutical company still conducting research on improved methods of birth control.[4] So, if I was serious about stopping at one child, this was where I belonged. For Sue, getting sterilized would have meant a real operation, real risk; for me it meant a bag of ice on my lap as I drove home. It all added up.

But there's no set of statistics to explain something else: why it felt odd, why it felt a little *shameful,* why it felt sad. Part of it is so deep inside, so encoded in my DNA, that I can't get at it. We were literally born to reproduce; the genes that encourage reproduction are the genes that get passed on from one generation to the next, amplified and strengthened over time. I remember several years ago sitting on a porch swing in the dark with my wife and one of my closest friends, talking about my reluctance to take this step, wondering about some of the same questions Dr. McGuire had asked me that morning. What if Sue and Sophie died in a plane crash, I found myself asking—what then? They chided me: surely I didn't think I could just replace my wife and child? And of course I didn't; if Sue and Sophie die in a plane crash, I hope I'm with them. Still, when I was honest, I could consciously sense the pull of my biology, the tidal tug to re-create myself. To remove that possibility goes against the grain of millions of years of our experience.

The technology of birth control, especially of permanent birth control, differs from the technologies we've embraced in the past. Fire, the wheel, the car, the airplane, the rocket-ship—those were all in line with our exuberant nature, our urge toward expansion. They were ways of extending our reach, making ourselves bigger. Vasectomy—that's a way of

making yourself smaller. Birth control is one of the few technologies that honors that other human gift, the one we share
with no other species, the gift of conscious self-restraint. It is
the technology of *less*. That's why it's different; that's why it's
spooky; that's why it's suspect.

That suspicion has worn many guises over time. National-
ists have opposed the idea of restraint, and Communists, and
capitalists wanting a giant market and a giant pool of labor.
But the deepest critique of restraint in childbearing has come
from people of faith. Since I am religious myself, a small-town
Methodist Sunday School teacher, I have no doubt that this
explains some of my uneasiness; in this overwhelmingly religious nation, it surely explains much of our queasiness in
even raising the topic. Most of our denominations no longer
condemn contraception, but even so there remains a sense
that it's a little shady. The condom ads still seem slightly out of
place on the tube. So we need to look with real care at the arguments from the faithful.

Too often these have been caricatured, twisted. "Given
that birth constitutes the major form of religious recruitment,"
writes one environmentalist, "it is not surprising that the di-
rigiste wings of all the world religions unite in encouraging
large families."[5] Such visions are common; in many minds the
pope appears to be the world's chief environmental criminal,
rashly urging large families in order to ensure the growth of
his empire. But those are canards, whether they're aimed at
Catholics or Hasidim or Mormons. The religious antipathy to
birth control has much richer and more profound roots, and it
is worth exploring them.

•   •   •

We are urged, on the first page of the first book of the Bible, to
be fruitful and multiply, to fill the earth. Since somewhat

more people begin reading the Bible than finish it, anything on the first page is bound to be influential. And indeed that injunction has created a mood, an *atmosphere*, that flavors the Judeo-Christian tradition; it gives the benefit of the doubt to fecundity. But it has not been by itself the key to the theological discussions of contraception. As David Feldman writes in his landmark study of Judaism and contraception, "no single Biblical passage, Talmudic precept, or rabbinic Responsum can convey the attitude of Judaism toward birth control."[6] Indeed, Feldman begins his book not with procreation but with marriage, which is a *mitzvah*, a religious duty. "It is not good for man to be alone," as the author of Genesis observed when describing the creation of Eve. "Therefore doth a man leave his father and mother and cleave unto his wife and they shall become as one flesh." Marriage is good in its own right, according to the sages, not simply as a boon to reproduction. And partly because it enhances marriage, sex is considered a great good, a duty owed by a husband to his wife.

But man, alone among the animals, can understand (and attempt to ward off) the results of sex; we are not like the other creatures, who are also told to be fruitful and multiply on the first page of Genesis. And so the Scriptures add other commandments to multiply. After Noah survives the flood, for instance, God commands him twice to be fruitful, and says the same to Jacob at Bethel.[7] It's sometimes called the "first mitzvah" of the Torah. As one fourteenth-century commentator says, "the purpose of this commandment is that the world be populated; it is a great mitzvah for, through it, all other commandments may be fulfilled."[8] A couple can discharge the obligation by bearing a boy and a girl—by replacing themselves—but the Talmud urges that parents keep going, if only to make sure that their children are not sterile, or don't die before reproducing *themselves*. As Maimonides wrote, man should not "desist from procreation while he yet has strength."[9] Among the most strictly observant, it is advice that still holds. Robert Eisenberg, in his travels among the ultra-Orthodox, describes sitting at a table in Brooklyn with seventeen Satmar Hasidim. "What's the largest family you know?" he asks the crowd. "Seventeen," one says. "No, twenty-one," another reminds him.[10]

Though worked out with all the marvelous intricacy of the Talmudic scholar, the Jewish understanding of birth control is relatively straightforward. It celebrates sex but not self-indulgence, and it has helped assure growth from a tiny band and survival against odds more daunting than any other race has ever faced. By contrast, the Christian understanding (which because of the wider spread of the faith and the political power of the various churches is more crucial to the mathematics of this topic) is infinitely stranger. The Gospels, which is to say Jesus, make scant comment on birth control or marriage or reproduction, but these became issues of great importance to early Christian thinkers.

The quick spread of the religion outside the confines of Judaism brought it into contact with practices of the Gentile world that alarmed its leaders, and with philosophies that influenced them. The use of contraceptives, for instance, was apparently fairly widespread in the Roman Empire (enough indeed that there was an official pronatalist policy designed to ensure a steady supply of soldiers, a policy reflected in the name given to the commoners: *proletarii*, or "breeders").[11] The Greek and Roman societies were hedonistic, sensual; against them were arrayed a variety of philosophies, especially Stoicism, that proclaimed asceticism as an ideal and preached renunciation of sex, marriage, and the family. Somewhere out of this mix came a celebration of celibacy, of virginity, most neatly summed up by Paul in his letter to the Church at Corinth. Asked by a convert if virginity is mandatory, he replies that it is good for a man not to touch a woman, that those widowed or not yet married should try to live a celibate life, but that for those who cannot control themselves, they should marry "for it is better to marry than to burn." He discusses marriage, and the sexual debt each partner owes the other, but nowhere in this crucial passage does he talk of procreation. And he stresses that even this discussion of marriage is a matter "of concession, not commandment."[12]

Paul should not be understood as a prude; he believes the end of time is near at hand, that judgment will come any day. He believes that his brethren are literally new creatures in Christ. But it is a mark of the radicalism of this new faith that Paul, born a Jew, should so thoroughly renounce the settled ideals of his tradition. As Notre Dame professor John Noonan wrote in his authoritative history of contraception and the Church, "it is the teaching on virginity which was a radical break from the Old Testament, and which put marriage in a place where, as it were, it had to justify its own existence."[13] The Church fathers simply were not very interested in offspring. Not only did they believe that the end was near, but their faith was spreading through proselytization, not procreation. The world was seen as full enough; Tertullian, the third-century theologian, even wrote that "pestilence, famine, wars, and earthquakes" were "blessings to overcrowded nations, since they serve to prune away the luxuriant growth of the human race."[14]

So the Church did not arrive at its condemnation of birth control out of a desire to produce more Christians, or in an effort to comply with the Genesis injunction to fill the world. Always—and in Catholicism to this day—it celebrated celibacy above all. And yet it did condemn contraception, condemn it in the strongest terms, from the third century through the end of the twentieth.

This paradox has several roots, but one of the most important lies in the reaction to the stew of heresies and splinter groups that haunted early Christianity. Consider the followers of Mani, who constituted a powerful third-century cult. They believed (like most religions) some wild things; their scriptures are filled with Ships of Light and with divine Virtues dressed up as beautiful maidens. You could liberate the trapped light of the Father by eating certain foods, and by certain kinds of sex; but procreation is "the evil act of evil," a perpetuation of the light's imprisonment.[15] And these Manichaeans managed to warp, albeit accidentally, the ways we still think about sex. That's because one of their early followers, Augustine, later converted to Christianity. St. Augustine laid down the most powerful early statements of Christian sexual ethics, and when he did so, he was reacting with the special zeal of an apostate against his earlier faith. Because the Manichaeans practiced birth control (apparently coitus interruptus), birth control was *wrong*. Procreation is not an imprisonment of the light, but a positive good; indeed in Augustine's view it becomes the sole reason for sex, and really for marriage. Those who, "by evil prayer or evil deed," obstruct procreation "although they are called husband or wife, are not; nor do they retain any reality of marriage, but with a respectable name cover a shame."[16]

Our attitudes might have turned out very differently, Noonan speculates, if later theologians had instead followed Augustine's contemporary, St. John Chrysostom, who was less fierce in his denunciations. Thomas Cahill, in his history of

Ireland, thought St. Patrick might have bred a Christianity less strict and more human.[17] But it was Augustine's influence that carried the day, and for a millennium the Church refined and deepened his abhorrence of contraception. For instance, the eighth-century writer known as Pseudo-Bede stipulated that murderers were required to do four years' penance by fasting on bread and water; contraceptors got a seven-year sentence. He even prescribed forty days of penance for sex with the woman on top, as this was thought to make conception less likely.[18]

Though the Manichaeans were eventually vanquished, new foes continued to arise. In the twelfth century, for example, it was the Troubadours, who in their songs—and their lives—developed an ideology of courtly love, "pure love" that embraced every kind of sex except insemination. (The word "bugger" entered our language at this time, because many members of this movement were from Bulgaria.)[19] Their attempt to divorce sex from procreation only hardened the orthodox Christian position, and certainly the primitive contraception of the time did little to slow the growth of population, which overcame even the plagues and wars that marked the period more deeply. Even the Protestant Reformation did not alter these attitudes, at least immediately. Luther didn't demand that ministers stay celibate; still, he calls marriage "a hospital for the sick. . . . I will not concede to nature that it is no sin."[20]

And yet, slowly but surely, some of the sternness began to erode, both within and without Catholicism. As long ago as the Renaissance, theologians started slowly and tentatively to develop new ideas about marriage and sex; pleasure and companionship begin to creep into the equation. In subsequent centuries new attitudes and new advances in contraceptive technology begin to appear, first in (Catholic) France, where the birthrate fell nearly 20 percent between 1770 and 1800.[21] At nearly the same moment, Malthus published his famous essay; though he called contraception "a violation of the marriage bed" which "clearly comes under the head of vice," his work nonetheless made it respectable to advocate birth control in subsequent decades.[22] By the late nineteenth century, there were organizations across Europe and America to spread contraceptive information, and soon there were international congresses on birth control and population, and eventually this influenced the churches. The Anglican Church, at its Lambeth Conference in 1930, adopted a resolution endorsing "a life of discipline and self-control lived in the power of the Holy Spirit" as the best method of birth control, but allowing "that other methods may be used."[23] They were eventually followed by virtually every other mainline Protestant denomination. Such reform did not spread immediately to the Vatican. In 1930, in fact, apparently in reaction to the Anglicans, Pope Pius XI issued *Casti Connubii*, reaffirming a total ban on artificial contraception and coitus interruptus. But even in Rome change was coming. After the war, his successor Pius XII endorsed the rhythm method of birth control, though right through John Paul II the Vatican has continued "to teach the moral unlawfulness of [artificial] contraception."[24]

In any event, the opposition of the Catholic Church has probably done little to slow the spread of contraception in modern times. The Vatican may have played a role in the Reagan administration's decision to cease most funding for international family-planning efforts,[25] but its preachings have not persuaded many Church members. Spain and Italy, the two historical pillars of Catholicism, have the lowest fertility rates on the planet. Fertility has fallen fairly quickly across much of

Catholic Latin America, especially in Brazil. In the United States, Catholics and Protestants give birth at the same rate. A 1992 Gallup poll showed that 87 percent of American Catholics believed couples should "follow their consciences" in deciding about modern forms of contraception,[26] and among young American Catholics, 98 percent believed that they could practice artificial birth control and still be good Catholics.[27] People have decided, for better or for worse, that the celibate and all-male hierarchy of the Church has little to teach them about such intimate matters.

So the Christian argument that began with Paul and Augustine has nearly died out. Why don't we just be done with it, call it all a superstition, and leave it be? Because, I think, there's something deeper there than the hysteria about flesh—there's actually a very good reason for some of this residue of uneasiness, even of shame, that surrounds birth control. People don't usually tell casual acquaintances about their vasectomies the way they do their kidney stones, partly because of our cultural squeamishness about sex, but partly because of the deeply ingrained sense that there's something inherently *selfish* about not being willing to have children. It's not as strong as the sense of selfishness that can attach itself to abortion, but it's there nonetheless, the real relic of our long theological wrestle with these issues. And it is not so easily dismissed as Augustine's anti-Manichaean zealotry. Condoms may not be sinful, but selfishness must be, if anything is. The children of small families are no more selfish than any other kids—but are the parents?

In a consumer society, where we've been drilled relentlessly in selfishness, it's a peril to take seriously. Jeanne Safer, in her book *Beyond Motherhood*, interviews dozens of men and women who have decided against children. I have no wish to judge them, for it's often an honorable decision, and no one should bear children who feels he or she can't cope with them. On the other hand, I have no wish to *become* them. Those she interviewed are selfish, and proudly; one New York literary agent describes herself as "an advocate of selfishness." Safer says she herself felt her biological clock ticking, but heard other clocks as well:

> My practice is just starting to take off—I'll lose all the momentum if I cut back to part-time. That summer I thought, it'll have to wait until after we get back from Bali and I'm no longer taking medication to prevent malaria. And what about the trip to Turkey we want to take next summer?[28]

She was, she said, "particularly aware that children would change my marriage drastically. . . . Parenthood, I believed, would certainly spell the end of our nightly candlelit sandalwood-scented bubble baths complete with silly bath toys, where we played like children in a deliciously adult incarnation." Not only that, "I realized that having a child of my own would force me to spend a great deal of time doing things I'd disliked; I'd never been crazy about children's birthday parties when I'd attended them years earlier, and a trip to the circus is my idea of purgatory."[29]

Safer found many like-minded folk. Sandra Singer, for instance, a photographer who moonlights as a belly dancer to "guarantee her allure" and who insists that "I've seen too many women who have children lose their sexuality as well as their identity. They let their bodies go, and they complain about their husband's sexual advances. I complain about the lack."[30] Safer reconciles herself to her decision not to have kids, and celebrates by giving her own belly-dancing performance. "Working through feelings about motherhood had unleashed hidden reserves of creativity and femininity, and I emerged liberated, energized, and strong," she reports. In fact, one night she dreams of a cantaloupe growing on a vine in her parents' garden in the middle of winter: "The cantaloupe was myself, the fruit of my parents' loins, which, though barren in the biological sense, was ripening out of season."[31]

It's wrong to ridicule such attitudes, at least in a culture that still assigns most women the work of raising kids while allowing men to continue their careers at full tilt. Sometimes people have to rescue themselves; in Toni Morrison's novel *Sula*, the heroine won't marry or bear children in order to preserve her "Me-ness." When her grandmother wants her to have babies to "settle" her, Sula says, "I don't want to make somebody else. I want to make myself."[32] Often it's women from very poor backgrounds who decide to remain childless, realizing that it's their best hope for upward mobility against strong odds. In a 1985 study of poor southern high school students, the 16 percent who wanted no children were the ones with the loftiest ambitions, the ambitions that in other contexts we want such children to have.[33]

But it's also possible to understand the concern of popes and rabbis and just ordinary folk that, for some people, the decision to have no children or a small family represents a decision to indulge yourself without a thought for anyone else, a decision to take sandalwood-scented candlelit baths without the danger that there might be stray Legos left in the tub to poke you in the backside. Gilbert Meilaender, a professor of religion at Oberlin, quotes one young man who says: "When you have children, the focus changes from the couple to the kids. Suddenly, everything is done for them. Well, I'm 27, I've used up a good portion of my life already. Why should I want to sacrifice for someone who's still got his whole life ahead of him?"[34] Such an attitude is, among other things, environmentally problematic; even if such a fellow has no kids, thereby sparing the planet some burden, he seems unlikely to do much else to ensure its future—he's likely the same guy who's going to be voting against gas taxes and demanding the right to drive his Suburban into the overheated sunset.

John Ryan, an American Catholic theologian of the first half of the twentieth century, made this argument most powerfully, I think, and in a completely different way than Augustine. A man of impeccable progressive credentials, Ryan was known as "the Right Reverend New Dealer" for his unwavering support of the Roosevelt administration. But this same John Ryan also wanted everyone who married to have many children, not simply as proof that they weren't using birth control but because he thought that raising large families made people better human beings. In several of his books he argues that supporting large families demanded "forms of discipline necessary for the successful life," a life "accomplished only at the cost of continuous and considerable sacrifice, of compelling ourselves to do without the immediate and pleasant goods for the sake of remote and permanent goods."[35] One of eleven children himself, Ryan thought that most people practicing birth control would be doing it from a "decadent" frame of mind; that bachelors were not building the kind of character necessary to contribute to the common good of society. Not only that, those with few children might become too wealthy, which was as dangerous as being too poor. In the words of ethicist John Berkman, "he was appealing to hard work, and building character, and he thought that was best achieved for most people in the context of having a large family."

This pragmatic argument comes straight from the American sense of purpose. And it is by no means a neglible or stupid argument: successfully raising a large brood of well-adjusted children is a great accomplishment, one that cannot help but change and deepen the parents. You emerge different people when you spend your life focusing, as good parents must, on *someone else's* well-being. Recall the definition of maturity we used earlier in the book: the realization that you are not at the center of the world. By that measure, *the most time-honored way to become mature is to be a parent many times over, and a good one.* Not just for the reason Ryan gives—because parenting is tough. But also because it's so *joyful,* because it shows you that real transcendent pleasure comes from putting someone else first. It teaches you how dull self-absorption can be.

Such lessons don't always take, of course. As the essayist Katha Pollitt points out, the tendency to ascribe "particular virtues—compassion, patience, common sense, nonviolence—to mothers" is an overdone, and in some ways oppressive, cliché;[36] and telling yourself that toilet training a string of two-year-olds is good for your soul may keep you away from other worlds. Furthermore, in a country where incredible numbers of fathers simply walk away from their kids, you could argue that fatherhood seems to barely dent the culture's pervasive selfishness. And yet when I think of my circle of friends and acquaintances, the single most common route to maturity has been through raising children, often lots of children.

The problem, of course, is that now we live in an era—maybe only a brief one, maybe only for a few generations—when parenting a bunch of kids clashes with the good of the planet. So is there a different way to achieve some of that maturity, with no children or only a single child to change your life? It's not that one kid won't alter most things in your life; he or she will. But Ryan was right—it's not the total commitment that comes with a large brood. Your career or your calling continues, however hobbled you may sometimes be. Alice Walker, in a pithy essay titled "*One* Child of One's Own," called her single daughter a "meaningful digression," and that's right in many ways; if she had borne *five* children, she probably wouldn't have been writing many books.[37] But those books represent a serious attempt at maturity in another way, and perhaps that's a clue. We need to find ways to be adults, grown-ups, *people who focus on others*, without being parents of large families.

In the weeks leading up to 1994's Cairo Conference on population, the pope led the fight against many of the provisions in the draft documents for that conclave. Though I disagreed with some of his stands, I found much of his language powerful and intriguing. The Church, he said one Sunday, does not support "an ideology of fertility at all costs," but instead an ethic in which the decision "whether or not to have a child" is not "motivated by selfishness or carelessness, but by a prudent, conscious generosity that weighs the possibilities and circumstances." True, he added that such an ethic "gives priority to the welfare of the unborn child," but several weeks later, arguing that radical individualism and "a sexuality apart from ethical references" was inhuman, he called for a "culture of responsible procreation."[38] In those words, and the words of many others, I think we can see the outline of an ethic that avoids self-indulgence and yet does not deny the physical facts of a planet with 6 billion people that may soon nearly double their numbers, a planet that grows hotter, stormier, and less stable by the day, a planet where huge swaths of God's creation are being wiped out by the one species told to tend this particular garden. I don't pretend it is an ethic that can be embraced by the Vatican, or the Hasidim; but I do think it is an ethic that might undergird a more sustainable world.

Return to the beginning of Genesis, to the fateful command, repeated elsewhere in the Hebrew Bible, that we are "to be fruitful, and multiply, and fill the earth." That this was the first commandment gave it special priority, as we have seen. And it was bio-logical, too, a command that echoed what our genes already shouted. But there is something else unique about it—it is the first commandment we have *fulfilled*. There's barely a habitable spot on the planet without a human being; more, in our lifetimes we've filled every inch of the planet with our *presence*. Everywhere the temperature climbs, the ultraviolet penetrates more deeply. In farthest Alaska, always our national metaphor for emptiness, the permafrost now melts at a rapid pace, trees move on to the tundra, insects infest forests in record numbers, and salmon turn back down streams because the water's gotten too warm to spawn. "There's been a permanent and significant climate regime shift," says one Alaskan scientist. "There has been nothing like this in the record."[39] There's not a creature anywhere on earth whose blood doesn't show the presence of our chemicals, not an ocean that isn't higher because of us. For better and for worse, we are everywhere. *We can check this commandment off the list.*

And we can check it off for happier reasons as well. There's no denying that we've done great environmental damage, but it's also true that we've spread wondrous and diverse cultures, full of love and song, across the wide earth. We should add a holiday to the calendar of every church, a day when we celebrate this achievement.

But when you check something off a list, you don't just

throw the list away. You look farther down the list, see what comes next. And the list, of course, is long. The Gospels, the Torah, the Koran, and a thousand other texts sacred and profane give us plenty of other goals toward which to divert some of the energy we've traditionally used in raising large families, goals on which we've barely begun. Feed the hungry, clothe the naked, comfort the oppressed; love your neighbor as yourself; heal the earth. We live on a planet where 3 billion people don't have clean water, where species die by the score each day, where kids grow up without fathers, where violence overwhelms us, where people judge each other by the color of their skin, where a hypersexualized culture poisons the adolescence of girls, where old people and young people need each other's support. *And the energy freed by having smaller families may be some of the energy needed to take on these next challenges*, to *really* take them on, not just to announce that they're important, or to send a check, or to read an article, but to make them central to our lives.

I have one child; she is the light of my life; she makes me care far more about the future than I used to. And I have one child; so even after my work I have some time left, and some money left, and some energy left, to do other things. I get to work on Adirondack conservation issues, and assist those who are fighting global warming; I've helped my wife start a new school in our town; I can teach Sunday School, and help run a nationwide effort to decommercialize Christmas, and sit on the board of the local college. (And I "belly-dance," too, though in my case it's hiking, cross-country skiing, mountain biking.) If I had three kids, I would still do those things, but less of them; either that or my work would come at their expense. As it is, once in a while I'm stretched too thin, and hardly see Sophie all day, and that reminds me to slow down, to find the real center of my life. But I do want to get farther down that list.

So the pope strikes me as largely right, in his reasoning if not his conclusions. Radical individualism *is* inhuman. Living as if you were the most important thing on earth is, literally, blasphemy; recreational sex may not bother me, but recreational *life* does. Our decisions *should* be motivated "not by selfishness or carelessness, but by a prudent conscious generosity." It's just that at the end of the twentieth century, on this particular planet, the signs of the times point me in the direction of the kinds of caring, the ways of maturing, that come with small, not large, families.

The Church should not find that argument so foreign. Priests are celibate, at least in part, because it allows them to make Christ their bride, to devote all their energies to the other tasks set before us on this earth. And the wisdom of that argument is proved daily in a million places around the globe where committed priests and nuns take on the hardest and dirtiest challenges the earth has to offer. If we now have plenty of people to guarantee our survival as a race, and if lots more people may make that survival harder, then it's time to follow the lead of those clerics a little—not to embrace celibacy necessarily, but to love your child to pieces, and with whatever you have left to start working your way down the list.

And the same logic should make it clear, of course, that all sorts of other kinds of people—childless gay people, infertile people, people who do not feel called to parenthood—can become every bit as mature (or immature) as a parent of six, as long as they can find some substitute discipline for repeatedly ranking someone or something else at the center of their lives. Sometimes those disciplines are quiet and private; sometimes public. In Allan Gurganus's recent novel of New York in the AIDS years, his main character describes taking care of one friend after another as they succumbed, describes the almost hydraulic outpouring of love it took to tend them. "My own loved ones were not brought into the world by me, but only, in my company, let out of it," he writes. His own obituary, he knows, will show that he left "no immediate survivors." "And yet I feel I've earned a family too." More so, of course, than many parents.[40]

* * *

When she began studying the differences between pro-choice and pro-life advocates in the abortion dispute, Kristin Luker noticed something interesting. It was true that they differed over the morality of terminating pregnancy, but those differences were the product of other, more fundamental, splits in their view of the world. They felt differently about God, about the role of women, and, most interestingly, they felt very differently about the nature of planning.

Pro-choice activists, she observed, were almost obsessed with planning for their children, trying to give them "maximum parental guidance and every possible advantage," while parents active in the antiabortion movement "tend to be laissez-faire individualists in their attitude" toward child rearing.[41] "Pro-life people," she wrote, "believe that one becomes a parent by *being* a parent; parenthood is for them a 'natural' rather than a social role.... The values implied by the invogue term *parenting* (as in *parenting classes*) are alien to them."[42] One woman that she interviewed said, "I think people are foolish to worry about things in the future. The future takes care of itself."[43] Too much planning, including too much family planning, means "playing God."

One of my favorite magazines comes from a small Ohio

town. Called *Plain*, it is edited (and its type hand-set) by "conservative" Quakers, which is to say a group of men and women who call themselves nonviolent Luddites and who live somewhat in the fashion of old-order Amish. The magazine recently reprinted a dinner conversation about the subject of family planning. The participants, each of them parents of four children, were discussing their unease with contraception, and in terms very reminiscent of Luker's study:

> MIRIAM: It breeds the mentality that "I want what I want, when I want."
>
> SCOTT: It leads back to self-seeking, which eventually knows no bounds.
>
> MARVIN: Actually, it leads to a bottom-line refusal to accept God's will for our lives.
>
> SCOTT: I think that one of the things Mary Ann and I have learned along the way, and which has further separated us from the mainstream culture, is the realization that we can always make room for one more. Because the room to be made is in our hearts.[44]

That way of seeing the world attracts me; there is in its spontaneity and confidence something of real beauty. It offers a kind of freedom. Not the freedom of unlimited options that we've come to idolize, but a freedom from constant worrying and fretting. Sometimes I hate the calculator instinct in me, the part of me that constantly weighs benefits and risks, the part that keeps me safe and solvent at the expense of experience. There is something incredibly attractive about the mystery of the next child, and the next; I'd love to meet them. I'd love to leave it to God, or to chance, or to biology, or to destiny, or to the wind. Part of me thinks those conservative Quakers, those pro-lifers, are unequivocally right.

The trouble is, there are now other ways to play God in this world, and *not* planning is one of them.

This was not always the case. In the Book of Job in the Hebrew Bible, God appears as a taunting voice from the whirlwind: "Where were you when I laid the foundations of the earth?" he asks Job. "Who shut up the sea with doors . . . and said here shall thy proud waves be stayed? . . . Who has cleft a channel for the torrents of rain, and a way for the thunderbolt?"[45] Job has no way to reply, and no need; the earth is infinitely bigger than he; how absurd he would look standing at the edge of the sea and trying to whistle up the waves. God—the world—was huge, and we were tiny. Creation dwarfed us.

But now there are so many of us, and we have done such a poor job of planning for our numbers, that for the first time we can answer God back. We can say: we set the boundaries of the ocean. If we keep heating the planet at our current pace, the seas will rise two feet in the next century. Even one foot will bring the water ninety feet farther inland across the typical American beach, drowning wetland and marsh. It's our lack of planning that changes the rainfall, that means more severe storms and worse flooding.

We no longer have the luxury of not planning; we're simply too big. We dominate the earth. When people first headed west across the Plains, they didn't need a zoning board; now Californians fight hard to try and channel and control growth lest they choke on it. In a crowded world, not planning has as many consequences as planning. This is a special time, and that turns everything on its head.

•   •   •

Or *almost* everything. It shouldn't change our free will, our ability to make our own decisions. I've argued strenuously that we've reached a moment when single-child families make sense as a cultural norm. But I do not think we should have some kind of government authority issue and enforce this edict. Control of one's body, the decision to reproduce, is far more sacred than, say, property rights; this is not *really* an issue like zoning.

And this needs saying, needs saying at some length. After all, the largest nation on earth has made single-child families an official policy, enforced by every arm of the government. Perhaps China had no choice; perhaps it was truly forced against the wall by a prospect of famine so unfathomable that it truly needed to coerce its citizens. But the cost has been enormously high. There are 36 million more males than females in China; by century's end, there will be a surplus of 70 million single men. And, as Luise Cardarelli points out in a 1996 analysis, "the betrayal of Chinese girls was inevitable once the one-child policy was adopted." Boys are an investment in the future—they work, they support their parents in old age, they ensure that the family line continues. But in China girls usually disappear into the husband's family; there's no return on the investment of raising them, only the drain of the dowry.[46] Hundreds of thousands of girl children are simply abandoned each year, many to die; Kay Johnson quotes from the note on one girl found in 1992 in Hunan:

> This baby girl is now 100 days old. She is in good health and has never suffered any illness. Due to the current political situation and heavy pressures that are too difficult to explain, we, who were her parents for these first days, cannot continue taking care of her. We can only hope that in this

world there is a kind-hearted person who will care for her.
Thank you.

In regret and shame, your father and mother.[47]

No parent, for any reason, should ever have to make a choice like that. But in China it's hard to avoid. In factories, family-planning workers monitor women to make sure they do not become pregnant. "We watch for women who start to eat less, or who get morning sickness," explained one Changzhou functionary. "If a woman isn't as active as she usually is, that's a sign of pregnancy. . . . No one has ever become pregnant without one of us finding out." Women who use IUDs are X-rayed periodically to make sure the coil remains in place;[48] elsewhere in China the homes of some peasants have literally been blown up as punishment for having extra children. "If you don't have your census card, your moving-population control card and your marriage card, the police will confiscate your boat," said one fisherman. "We have all seen it."[49]

And it's not just in China, not just in places with flat-out bans on second and third children. You can find abuses in almost every spot where governments have pushed coercive quotas. Betsy Hartmann, in her book *Reproductive Rights and Wrongs*, travels around Asia looking at programs that some international family planners consider models, and finds constant horrors: woman pressured to install IUDs or take shots of Depo-Provera without adequate screening or supervision or follow-up; sterilization pressed on the unwilling.[50] In Peru, according to Steven Mosher, women are offered fifty pounds of food in return for submitting to a tubal ligation, and government doctors must meet a quota of six sterilizations a month or lose their jobs.[51]

Coercion is wrong; that would be reason enough to oppose it. But it's often counterproductive, too. Look at India, where the government of Indira Gandhi panicked in the 1970s and began trying to raise the rate of sterilization dramatically. They set up "vasectomy camps" throughout the nation, which I suspect were somewhat less well appointed than the Ottawa office I visited, and to round up "volunteers," they started withholding licenses for shops and cars, refusing to grant food ration cards, shutting off irrigation water. It "worked," in that 8.3 million men were sterilized in 1976. But it outraged everyone, cost Gandhi the next election—and it took another ten years for the level of contraceptive use to get back even to former levels. Meanwhile, the population kept growing.[52] China may face precisely the same kinds of problems; as the country becomes a little more free, people are starting to buy their way out of population controls.[53] The average Chinese, that is, may not have changed his mind about what constitutes a nice-sized family; there may be lots and lots and lots of pent-up demand.

Such coercion may have been unnecessary, too. Consider the example of India's southernmost state, Kerala, a province of 30 million people, as many as California. Though it is no richer than the rest of India, its population growth has virtually stopped; the fertility rate is lower than China's, lower than America's. And not because the government has forced anyone, or imposed special taxes, or given special favors to those with small families; the family-planning office in the capital city of Trivandrum is a dusty backwater, not a well-funded or powerful bureaucracy. No, the birthrate has fallen because there's plenty of health care, so that an infant death is now a rarity and people can count on their children to survive; it has fallen because there's plenty of education—the state has the highest literacy rate on earth for both men and women. It has fallen because there's been a real discussion in the society about what makes sense in that crowded place. "Seven or eight years ago the norm was three children, and we thought we were doing pretty good," M. N. Sivaram, the local representative of the International Family Planning Association, told me as we sat in his office, surrounded by the kind of family-planning posters you can find across the Third World. "Now it's two, and among the most educated people it's one."[54]

That's the kind of conversation we need here, far more than we need the kind of complicated schemes that some environmentalists have proposed. Garrett Hardin, for instance, suggested that "the relatively infertile might be rewarded with prestigious subsidized vacations";[55] while Kenneth Boulding urged a "system of marketable licenses" that the "rich and the philoprogenitive" could purchase from "the poor, the nuns, the maiden aunts, and so on."[56] Herman Daly and John Cobb urge "transferable birth quotas," perhaps with forcible adoption of any child born to parents who have not managed to acquire the necessary licenses.[57] Those schemes contain within them the seeds of a very different society than the one in which we live; given the choice between 400 million free Americans and 230 million cowed ones living in fear that the Birth Control Police might be coming to inspect their nurseries, I know which I'd choose.

More than that, though, such schemes make no sense, at least in a democratic society. If the day ever arrived that our politicians were willing to pass such legislation, that would be the same day on which they were no longer needed. Bill Clinton, or any other president in this poll-driven age, would sign such a law only once the vast majority of Americans supported it, at which point presumably the birthrate would already have fallen. Even with wide support, such laws would be wrong; this is not the kind of decision majorities should foist on minorities. But the point, in any event, is that we *have to have the conversation first*. We need to talk—with our spouses, with our parents, with our grandparents, with our scientists and our economists and our theologians. With *ourselves*—how many children we plan to have is one of those decisions we often leave in the back of our minds, often "decide" by accident or age. It needs to be a *conversation*, not an exchange of slogans.

We need to get over being so shy about it. We need to get over thinking about population as an abstract issue, a matter of "birthrates." Population is a matter of how many children each of us chooses to have, and at the moment that choice is as likely to be influenced by the nagging of grandparents ("she needs a playmate") and the nagging of myth ("only children are SPOILED") as by careful, steady thought. No decision any of us makes will have more effect on the world (and on our lives) than whether to bear another child. No decision, then, should be made with more care.

One of the arguments that occurs to most people as they think about their contribution to the world's population goes like this: it's true that each child places some additional burden on the earth, but perhaps some one of these children will invent something or make some discovery that will "solve our problems." This notion may have its flaws. Some have pointed out that Athens, with its 50,000 citizens, displayed more genius, and colonial America, with its 5 million, more political courage than our huge land. Greatness results not just from raw numbers, but some interaction between people, time, and place. Still, it's a sweet hope, this hope that any child in any maternity ward might hold the key to our troubles.

The problem, though, is that it relies on a kind of magical thinking. It depends on the idea that there's some new technology (cold fusion!) or some new method of organization (Marxism!) that can vaporize our problems. It depends, in other words, on the idea that we simply need to make one more, or two more, or a hundred more leaps in the same direction that we've been leaping. That we need another set of technologies to replace the old ones, technologies that will allow us to dominate everything around us but with more efficiency, less waste, less mess.

It's possible, however, that the geniuses have long since been born who offered us the necessary advice—that it's on the shelf and we just haven't gotten around to using it. The long line of gurus and cranks that runs back at least to the Buddha and the Christ suggested that we see the world in a slightly different way. They understood that the thing which makes us most fully human is not our capacity for restless expansion, for aggression and growth and domination (all of which we share with many other animals), but our capacity for self-restraint, for a kind of humility. That by making ourselves somewhat smaller we make ourselves truly human, just as fish make themselves fish by swimming, and birds by flying, and mosquitoes by biting.

The technologies of restraint are many: the bicycle, the spoken word, the hand offered in friendship and in help. And, in this time and this place, the technologies of contraception. They can be used as technologies of indulgence and self-obsession, but they can be the technologies of humility as well.

•   •   •

And tonight she went gracefully to bed. It was a wonderful afternoon: we stacked firewood together, and she rode on the wheelbarrow, and then we did a thing called "twisters" that Mom is not allowed to see, where you wind up the ropes of the swing and then it unwinds really fast even as you're going back and forth. Scrambled eggs for dinner, and then a chapter from one of the Narnia books. We sang "Amazing Grace," and told stories, and brushed teeth, and had hugs, several hugs.

Acknowledgments

M*any people helped with this book, though they should not be im-*
plicated in its conclusions. I am most grateful to Carl Haub of
the Population Reference Bureau, Professor Toni Falbo of the
University of Texas, Peter Raven, Kate Fish, Alan Durning, and
a host of journalists whose work has been especially helpful to
me, including Nick Kristof and William K. Stevens. Librarians
Russell Puschak and Kate Gardner assisted tremendously with
my research; I am also grateful to the Johnsburg Public Library
and the Southern Adirondack Library System. Sue Parilla,
Corby Kummer, and Bill Whitworth of *The Atlantic* were of
great assistance to me, as were Katy Roberts and Adam Moss
of *The New York Times*, Patti Wolter of *Mother Jones*, and Debo-
rah Bendis of the *Christian Century*.

This book required many good friends to bounce ideas off
of—they include Sam and Lisa Verhovek, Jonathan Rubin-
stein and Linda Motzkin, Shawn Leary and Michael Consi-

dine, Barbara Lemmel and Mitch Hay, Lisa Spilde and Mike Dabroski, and Jackie and Nick Avignon. (Jackie made this book possible in many other ways, too.) I am grateful to the students of the Mill Creek Methodist Sunday School, to my coteachers Sam and Sue Allison and Colleen Scheffold, and to our music director Betty Coulter. I am also grateful to the students and staff of the Wilderness Community School, especially Jenna Stauffer, Stephen Sexton, and Dee Warner.

My agent, Gloria Loomis, worked her usual wonders with this book, as did David Rosenthal and Annik LaFarge; I am so glad to be working with them, as well as with their colleagues Zoe Wolff, Victoria Meyer, Fred Wiemer, Steve Messina, and the rest of the Simon & Schuster staff.

My parents and my brother gave important love and guidance. My wife Sue was a partner in this as in every project, and as always my chief joy and support. And Sophie was—Sophie, which is so much that I can't even begin to say it.

Notes

PART ONE: FAMILY

Chapter One

1. Toni Falbo, "Only Children: A Review," in Toni Falbo, ed., *The Single-Child Family* (New York: Guilford Press, 1984), pp. 1–24.
2. Susan Newman, *Parenting an Only Child: The Joys and Challenges of Raising Your One and Only* (New York: Doubleday, 1990), pp. 22–23.
3. Saul Rosenzweig, *Freud, Jung, and Hall the Kingmaker* (Kirkland, Wash.: Hoagrefe & Hecher, 1992), pp. 64–65.
4. Ibid., p. 81.
5. Dorothy Ross, *G. Stanley Hall: The Psychologist as Prophet* (Chicago: University of Chicago Press, 1972), pp. 126–27.
6. Ibid., p. 300.
7. Ibid., pp. 294–95.
8. Ibid., p. 300.
9. Rosenzweig, p. 81.

10. E. W. Bohannon, "A Study of Peculiar and Exceptional Children," *Pedagogical Seminary* 4, no. 1 (1896): 3–60.

11. E. W. Bohannon, "The Only Child in a Family," *Pedagogical Seminary* 6, no. 2 (1898): 475.

12. G. Stanley Hall, "Boy Life in a Massachusetts Country Town Thirty Years Ago," *Proceedings of the American Antiquarian Society* 7 (1892): 107.

13. Ross, pp. 126–27.

14. Bohannon, "The Only Child," p. 493.

15. Norman Fenton, "The Only Child," *Journal of Genetic Psychology* 35 (1928): 546–47.

16. Judith Blake, *Family Size and Achievement* (Berkeley: University of California Press, 1989), p. 6.

17. Erica Goode, "Cracking the Myth of the Pampered, Lonely Misfit," *U.S. News & World Report*, January 10, 1994.

18. Newman, p. 186.

19. Dorothy Stein, "Childbearing," *Real World*, Spring 1993, p. 1.

20. Michael Lewis and Candice Feiring, "Some American Families at Dinner," in L. M. Laosa and M. E. Sigel, eds., *Families as Learning Environments for Children* (New York: Plenum Press, 1982).

21. Newman, p. 40.

22. Blake, p. 65.

23. Nicholas Zill and James Peterson, "Learning to Do Things Without Help," in Laosa and Sigel, eds., *Families as Learning Environments*, p. 356.

24. Blake, p. 65.

25. H. Theodore Groat, Jerry W. Wicks, and Arthur G. Neal, "Without Siblings: The Consequences in Adult Life of Having Been an Only Child," in Falbo, ed., *The Single-Child Family*.

26. Toni Falbo and Denise Polit, "A Quantitative Review of the Only Child Literature: Research Evidence and Theory Development," *Psychological Bulletin* 100 (1986): 176–89.

27. Blake, p. 11.

28. Ibid., p. 230.

29. Ibid., p. 11.

30. Laosa and Sigel, eds., *Families as Learning Environments*, p. 118.

31. Candice Feiring and Michael Lewis, "Only and First-Born Chil-

dren: Differences in Social Behavior and Development," in Falbo, ed., *The Single-Child Family*, p. 28.

32. Ibid.
33. Blake, p. 270.
34. Falbo and Polit, "A Quantitative Review."
35. Lewis and Feiring, "Some American Families at Dinner," pp. 115–34.
36. Feiring and Lewis, "Only and First-Born Children," p. 45.
37. Newman, p. 52.
38. Frank B. Gilbreth, Jr., and Ernestine Gilbreth Carey, *Cheaper by the Dozen* (New York: Crowell, 1948), p. 136.
39. Lincoln Day, *Journal of Applied Social Psychology* 21 (1991): 754.
40. Falbo, "Only Children," p. 3.
41. Newman, pp. 96–97.
42. Darrell Sifford, *The Only Child* (New York: Putnam, 1989), p. 65.
43. Toni Falbo, interview, March 27, 1997.
44. Denise F. Polit and Toni Falbo, "Only Children and Personality Development: A Quantitative Review," *Journal of Marriage and the Family* 49 (1987): 309.
45. Falbo, "Only Children."
46. Falbo, ed., *The Single-Child Family*.
47. Blake, p. 11.
48. Ibid., p. 229.
49. Newman, p. 25.
50. Blake, p. 254.
51. Ibid., p. 231.
52. Newman, p. 33.
53. Blake, pp. 231–32.
54. Phyllis A. Katz and Sally L. Boswell, "Sex-Role Development and the One-Child Family," in Falbo, ed., *The Single-Child Family*, p. 67.
55. John G. Claudy, "The Only Child as a Young Adult: Results from Project Talent," in Falbo, ed., *The Single-Child Family*.
56. Blake, p. 231.
57. Falbo, ed., *The Single-Child Family*.
58. Groat, Wicks, and Neal, "Without Siblings."
59. Day, pp. 754–73.

Chapter Two

1. Patrick E. Tyler, "As Pampered Generation Grows Up, Chinese Worry," *New York Times*, June 25, 1994, p. A1.
2. Toni Falbo, interview, March 26, 1997.
3. Toni Falbo and Dudley L. Poston, Jr., "The Academic, Personality, and Physical Outcomes of Only Children in China," in *Child Development* 64 (1993): 19–35.
4. Dudley L. Poston, Jr., and Toni Falbo, "Academic Performance and Personality Traits of Chinese Children: 'Onlies' versus 'Others,'" *American Journal of Sociology* 96, no. 2 (1990): 433.
5. Falbo, interview.
6. Robert Boynton, "Birth of An Idea," *New Yorker*, October 7, 1996.
7. Alan Wolfe, "Up from Scientism: What Birth Order Can't Explain," *New Republic*, December 23, 1996.
8. Robin Estrin, "Birth Order May Affect Traits," Associated Press, October 14, 1996.
9. Wolfe, "Up from Scientism," p. 22.
10. Frank Sulloway, *Born to Rebel* (New York: Pantheon, 1996), p. 204.
11. Ibid., p. 234.
12. Ibid., p. 503.
13. Falbo, interview.
14. Goode, "Cracking the Myth."
15. Ibid.
16. Stephen Bank and Michael Kahn, *The Sibling Bond* (New York: Basic Books, 1982), p. 3.
17. Ibid., pp. 8–9.
18. Ibid., p. 19.
19. Goode, "Cracking the Myth."
20. Bank and Kahn, pp. 198–99.
21. Falbo, "Only Children."
22. Rita Kramer, *In Defense of the Family* (New York: Basic Books, 1983), pp. 80–81.
23. Bank and Kahn, p. 205.
24. Goode, "Cracking the Myth."

25. Judy Dunn and Robert Plomin, *Separate Lives: Why Siblings Are So Different* (New York: Basic Books, 1990), pp. 106–7.
26. Bank and Kahn, p. 33.
27. Ibid., pp. 169–70.
28. Dunn and Plomin, p. 158.
29. Ibid., pp. 80–81.
30. Ibid., p. 167.
31. Ibid., pp. 74–75.
32. But not my mom.
33. Dunn and Plomin, p. 63.
34. Ibid., pp. 78–79.
35. Ibid., pp. 86–87.
36. Philip Larkin, "This Be the Verse," in Angela Partington, ed., *The Oxford Dictionary of Quotations*, p. 410.
37. Bank and Kahn, p. 13.
38. Nicholas Eberstadt, "World Population Implosion," *Public Interest*, 1997.
39. Frederic Wiegold, ed., *The Wall Street Journal Lifetime Guide to Money* (New York: Hyperion Books, 1997), pp. 252–53.
40. Katz and Boswell, "Sex Role Development," p. 63.
41. Groat, Wicks, and Neal, "Without Siblings," p. 258.

PART TWO: SPECIES

Chapter Three

1. Ecclesiastes 1:4, 9–10 (New Revised Standard Version).
2. Lamont C. Hempel, "Roots and Wings," League of Women Voters Population Coalition, White Paper no. 3, 1996.
3. Lester Brown and Hal Kane, *Full House: Reassessing the Earth's Population Carrying Capacity* (New York: Norton, 1994), p. 51.
4. "World Growth Rate Slows, but Numbers Build Up," *Population Today*, November 1994, p. 1.
5. Carl Haub, interview, January 31, 1997. (Numbers quoted exclude China.)
6. "Population Growth Rate Slows," *Population Today*, January 1994, p. 1.

7. Barbara Crossette, "World Is Less Crowded Than Expected, the U.N. Reports," *New York Times*, November 17, 1996, p. 3.

8. Joel E. Cohen, *How Many People Can the Earth Support?* (New York: Norton, 1995), p. 367.

9. Lester Brown, "Facing Food Security," *Earth Island Journal*, Spring 1997, p. 38.

10. Cohen, p. 32.

11. Lincoln H. Day and Alice Taylor Day, *Too Many Americans* (Boston: Houghton Mifflin, 1964), p. 5.

12. Haub, interview.

13. "Model Shows How Medical Changes Let Population Surge," *New York Times*, January 17, 1997, p. A16.

14. Farzaneh Roudi, "Spotlight Oman," *Population Today*, May 1997, p. 1.

15. Nicholas Eberstadt, "The Premises of Population Policy: A Reexamination," in Michael Cromartie, ed., *The Nine Lives of Population Control* (Grand Rapids: Eerdmans, 1995), p. 30.

16. Ibid., p. 23.

17. Haub, interview.

18. Ben Wattenberg, "The Population Explosion Is Over," *New York Times Magazine*, November 23, 1997, p. 61.

19. William R. Catton, Jr., "The World's Most Polymorphic Species," *Bioscience* 37, no. 6 (1987).

20. Ben Bolch and Harold Lyons, *Apocalypse Not* (Washington, D.C.: Cato Institute, 1993).

21. Garrett Hardin, *Living Within Limits: Ecology, Economics, and Population Taboos* (New York: Oxford University Press, 1993), p. 120.

22. Mathis Wackernagel and William E. Rees, *How Big Is Our Ecological Footprint?* (Vancouver: University of British Columbia Press, 1993), p. 8.

23. Lester Brown, *The Agricultural Link: How Environmental Deterioration Could Disrupt Environmental Progress* (Washington, D.C.: Worldwatch Paper 136, 1997), p. 10.

24. Julian Simon and Karl Zinsmeister, "How Population Growth Affects Human Progress," in Cromartie, ed., *The Nine Lives*, p. 67.

25. Nathan Keyfitz, "Population and Development Within the

Ecosphere: One View of the Literature," *Population Index* 57, no. 1.

26. Paul Harrison, *The Third Revolution: Population, Environment, and a Sustainable World* (New York: Penguin, 1993), pp. 13–14.

27. Bill McCormick, "Is Population Control Genocide?" *Wild Earth*, Spring 1991, p. 4.

28. J. Mayone Stycos, "The Second Great Wall of China," *Population and Environment* 12, no. 4 (1991).

29. Simon and Zinsmeister, "Population Growth," p. 67.

30. Fairfield Osborn, *The Limits of the Earth* (Boston: Little, Brown, 1953).

31. Julian Simon, *The Ultimate Resource* (Princeton, N.J.: Princeton University Press, 1981), p. 56.

32. Paul R. Ehrlich, prologue to *The Population Bomb* (New York: Ballantine, 1968).

33. William Bender and Margaret Smith, *Population, Food, and Nutrition* (Washington, D.C.: Population Reference Bureau, 1997).

34. Brown, *The Agricultural Link*, p. 15.

35. Harrison, pp. 14–15.

36. Ester Boserup, *Population Size and Technological Development* (Chicago: University of Chicago Press, 1981).

37. Simon and Zinsmeister, "Population Growth," p. 74.

38. Simon, p. 348.

39. Ed Regis, "Julian Simon, the Doomslayer," *Wired*, February 1997.

40. Ben Wattenberg, *The Good News Is That the Bad News Is Wrong* (New York: Simon & Schuster, 1984), p. 95.

41. Peter Vitousek, interview, September 16, 1997.

42. David Pimentel, interview, December 3, 1996.

43. Pimentel et al., "Environmental and Economic Costs of Soil Erosion," *Science*, February 24, 1995.

44. Pimentel, interview.

45. Robert Engelman and Pamela Leroy, *Conserving Land* (Washington, D.C.: Population Action International, 1995), p. 20.

46. *Greenwire*, Web site, published by *National Journal*, March 25, 1997.

47. Sandra Postel, "Where Have All the Rivers Gone," *Worldwatch Magazine* 8, no. 3 (May–June 1995): p. 9.

48. Sandra Postel, *Dividing the Waters* (Washington, D.C.: World-watch Institute, 1996) p. 7.

49. Ibid., pp. 12–13.

50. Pimentel, interview.

51. Simon, p. 71.

52. Brown, *The Agricultural Link*, p. 25.

53. Charles Mann, "Reseeding the Green Revolution," *Science*, August 22, 1997, p. 1038.

54. William Catton, "Carrying Capacity and the Death of a Culture: A Tale of Two Autopsies," *Sociological Inquiry* 63, no. 2 (1993): 202.

55. Ibid., p. 59.

56. William Catton, *Overshoot: The Ecological Basis of Revolutionary Change* (Urbana: University of Illinois Press, 1982), p. 7.

57. William Catton, "Can Irrupting Man Remain Human?" *BioScience* 26, no. 4 (1986).

58. William E. Rees and Mathis Wackernagel, "Ecological Footprints and Appropriated Carrying Capacity," in Ann-Mari Jansson, ed., *Investing in Natural Capital* (Washington, D.C.: Island Press, 1994).

59. Cohen, p. 367.

60. Carl Safina, *Song for the Blue Ocean* (New York: Holt, 1997), p. 2.

61. Jeff Regnart, interview, July 21, 1997.

62. Lester Brown, interview, August 1, 1997.

Chapter Four

1. Simon, p. 22.

2. Lester Brown, *Vital Signs* (New York: Norton/Worldwatch Institute, 1996), p. 19.

3. Mark Hertsgaard, "Who's Afraid of Global Warming," *Washington Post*, January 21, 1996.

4. George Perkins Marsh, *Man and Nature* (Cambridge, Mass.: Harvard University Press, 1973), p. 3.

5. B. L. Turner, ed., *The Earth as Transformed by Human Beings: Global and Regional Changes in the Biosphere over the Last Three Hundred Years* (New York: Cambridge University Press, 1993).

6. Brown, *Vital Signs*, p. 75.

7. Turner, p. 8.

8. Ibid., p. 19.

9. "Reservoirs May Be Altering Speed of Earth's Orbit," *Raleigh News and Observer*, March 3, 1996, p. 13A.

10. Peter M. Vitousek et al., "Human Domination of Earth's Ecosystems," *Science*, July 25, 1997.

11. Vaclav Smil, "Global Population and the Nitrogen Cycle," *Scientific American*, July 1997, p. 76.

12. William K. Stevens, "Too Much of a Good Thing Makes Benign Nitrogen a Triple Threat," *New York Times*, December 10, 1996, p. C1.

13. Bill McKibben, *The End of Nature* (New York: Random House, 1989), p. 17.

14. Outside Online, "U.S. Air Quality Improves Despite Increased Traffic," April 22, 1997.

15. William K. Stevens, "Talk About Weather: U.N. Says People Do Something About It," *New York Times*, December 1, 1995.

16. Richard Cole, "Experts: Bad Storms on the Rise," Associated Press, January 18, 1997.

17. William K. Stevens, "Blame Global Warming for the Blizzard," *New York Times*, February 19, 1996.

18. William K. Stevens, "Experts on Climate Change Ponder: How Urgent Is It?" *New York Times*, September 9, 1997, p. C1.

19. Cole, "Experts," p. 1.

20. Glenda Chui, "Global Warming Blamed for Ever Earlier Spring," *San Jose Mercury News*, July 11, 1996, p. 1.

21. "Earth 'Breathing' Deeper, Spring Coming Earlier," *Atmosphere Alliance News*, Fall 1996, p. 1.

22. Chui, "Global Warming," p. 3.

23. Matt Crenson, "Spring Comes Early to Arctic," Associated Press, April 16, 1997.

24. Joby Warrick, "Spring Sprouting Earlier Than a Decade Ago," *Washington Post*, April 17, 1997, p. A12.

25. Thomas Karl, Ozone Action Roundtable, National Press Club, June 24, 1996.

26. William K. Stevens, "Greener Grain Belt Bears Witness to Warming Trend," *New York Times*, April 22, 1997, p. C1.

27. Brown, *The Agricultural Link*, p. 15.

28. "Scientists Say Earth's Warming Could Cause Widespread Disruptions," *New York Times,* September 18, 1995, p. C1.

29. Ellen Mosley-Thompson, "Current Effects of Climate Change," Ozone Action Roundtable, National Press Club, June 24, 1996.

30. American Association of Geographers, press release, April 1997, on the @IGC Web site.

31. Wendy Hower, "Life at the Lake: Scientists Study Global Warming North of the Arctic Circle," *Fairbanks Daily News-Miner,* July 14, 1996, p. 1.

32. Eugene Linden, "Warnings from the Ice," *Time,* April 14, 1997, p. 54.

33. Ibid., p. 57.

34. Rauber, "Heat Wave," p. 39.

35. Danny Westreat, "Experts: Northwest Warming Rapidly," *Seattle Times,* October 16, 1996, p. 1.

36. Nicholas Kristof, "In Pacific, Growing Fears of Paradise Engulfed," *New York Times,* March 2, 1997, p. A1.

37. Kevin E. Trenberth, "What's Happening to El Niño," *Encyclopaedia Britannica 1996 Book of the Year,* p. 164.

38. "Arctic Tundra Is Leaking More Carbon—Scientists," Reuters, December 17, 1996.

39. Linden, "Warnings," p. 57.

40. Stefan Rahmstorf, "Ice Cold in Paris," *New Scientist,* February 1997.

41. Linden, "Warnings," p. 57.

42. "Chicago Heat Toll Raised," *New York Times,* September 22, 1995.

43. "Global Warming–Malaria Link," Associated Press, July 10, 1996.

44. Norman Myers, "Environmental Refugees in a Globally Warmed World," *BioScience* 43, no. 11 (1993): 752.

45. Norman Myers, *Ultimate Security: The Environmental Basis of Political Stability* (New York: Norton, 1993), pp. 198–99.

46. Engelman and Leroy, p. 20.

47. Rosamond Naylor et al., "Variability and Growth in Grain Yields, 1950–1994," *Population and Development Review* 23, no. 1 (March 1997): 55.

48. Ross Gelbspan, "The Heat Is On," *Harper's*, December 1996, p. 24.
49. Ed Regis, "Julian Simon, the Doomslayer," *Wired*, February 1997, p. 71.
50. John Passacantando, interview, August 18, 1997.

Chapter Five

1. Ehrlich, p. 15.
2. Amartya Sen, 1995, "Population, Delusion, and Reality," in Michael Cromartie, ed., *The Nine Lives of Population Control* (Grand Rapids: Eerdmans, 1995), p. 105.
3. Paul R. Ehrlich, Anne H. Ehrlich, and Gretchen Daily, *The Stork and the Plow* (New York: Putnam, 1995), p. 25.
4. Victoria Dompka, *Population and the Environment* (Washington, D.C.: World Wildlife Fund, 1995), p. 20.
5. Alan Durning, *How Much Is Enough?* (New York: Norton, 1992), p. 50.
6. Charles Hall et al., "The Environmental Consequences of Having a Baby in the United States," *Wild Earth*, Summer 1995, p. 78.
7. Paul Harrison, frontispiece in *The Third Revolution: Population, Environment, and a Sustainable World* (New York: Penguin, 1993).
8. Odil Tunali, "Carbon Emissions Hit All-Time High," in Brown, *Vital Signs*, p. 64.
9. Bill McKibben, *Hope, Human and Wild* (Boston: Little, Brown, 1995).
10. "No Evasion on Greenhouse Gases," editorial, *Boston Globe*, June 30, 1997.
11. Ozone Action, "U.S. Carbon Emissions Now Projected to Grow to 15.4 Percent over 1990 Levels by 2000," pamphlet, January 1997.
12. Draft Second National Communication, U.S. Department of State, *Federal Register* 62, no. 91 (May 12, 1997): 25988–89.
13. Westreat, "Exports."
14. *Global Warming Today*, January 4, 1996, p. 1.

15. "Climate Change: Australia May Withdraw from Pact," *Greenwire*, May 5, 1997.

16. Robert Goodland, Herman E. Daly, and Salah El Serafy, *Population, Technology, and Lifestyle: The Transition to Sustainability* (Washington, D.C.: Island Press, 1992), p. 4.

17. Paul Hawken, "Hypercar," *Mother Jones*, March–April 1997, p. 52.

18. "Electric Vehicles: General Motors Cuts EV1 Price by 25%," *Greenwire*, May 3, 1997.

19. Coalition for Vehicle Choice, Web site, December 1996.

20. Matthew Wald, "Junked Vehicles Outperform New Models," *New York Times*, August 11, 1997, p. D1.

21. Robyn Meredith, "Sales Results Show Americans Buying Trucks and More Trucks," *New York Times*, September 4, 1997, p. 15.

22. Keith Bradsher, "Start Expanding That Garage for Detroit's Next Generation," *New York Times*, June 17, 1997, p. A1.

23. Agis Salpukas, "Fast Speeds and Big Cars Send Gas Consumption Up," *New York Times*, February 15, 1996, p. D1.

24. Matthew Wald, "Number of Cars Is Growing Faster than Human Population," *New York Times*, September 21, 1997, p. D1.

25. Ibid., p. D3.

26. "Mountaineer Breaks Code of Silence," *USA Today*, April 10, 1996, p. 5B.

27. Salpukas, "Fast Speeds," p. D5.

28. Roy Beck, *Recharting America's Future* (Petoskey, Mich.: Social Contract Press, 1994), p. 39.

29. "Quote of the Month," Coalition for Vehicle Choice Web site, September–October 1996.

30. Neva R. Goodwin, Frank Ackerman, and David Kiron, eds., *The Consumer Society* (Washington, D.C.: Island Press, 1996), p. 3.

31. Kevin Kelly and Gary Wolf, "Push: The Radical Future of Media Beyond the Web," *Wired*, March 1997.

32. McKibben, *Hope*, p. 53.

33. Bernard Wysocki, Jr., "In Developing Nations, Many Youths Splurge, Mainly on U.S. Goods," *Wall Street Journal*, June 26, 1997, p. 1.

34. Vicki Robin, *All Consuming Passion* (Seattle: New Road Map, 1996).

35. David G. Myers, "Does Economic Growth Improve Human Morale?" *Enough* 1, no. 1 (Summer 1997): 1.

36. Dana Canedy, "Quality, Not Flash, Marks New Gains in Luxury Sales," *New York Times*, December 12, 1996, p. A1.

37. Trip Gabriel, "Six Figures of Fun—It's Bonus Season on Wall Street," *New York Times*, February 12, 1997, p. D1.

38. Canedy, "Quality, Not Flash," p. A1.

39. Julie V. Iovine, "Padding the Empty Nest: Couples Build Bigger as Their Children Leave Home," *New York Times*, September 4, 1997, p. C1.

40. Anthony Faiola, "Runoff from the Rain Forest," *Washington Post*, January 2, 1997, p. D12.

41. Bruce Selcraig, "Albuquerque Learns It Really Is a Desert Town," *High Country News*, December 26, 1994, p. 1.

42. Arthur Rypinski, interview, May 28, 1997.

43. Andrew Rudin, "The Inefficiencies of Efficiency," *Public Power*, May–June 1995, p. 20.

44. Andrew Rudin, "Comfort and Light," *Newsletter of the Interfaith Coalition on Energy*, no. 61 (Spring 1996).

45. Mobil Oil, "Climate Change: We're All in This Together," *New York Times*, advertisement, 1996.

46. President's Council on Sustainable Development, "Sustainable America: A New Consensus," February 1996.

47. Rypinski, interview.

48. Ibid.

49. Gar Smith, "Buick Does Beijing," *Earth Island Journal*, Spring 1997, p. 6.

50. Patrick Tyler, "China's Inevitable Dilemma—Coal Equals Growth," *New York Times*, November 29, 1995, p. A1.

51. Ian Johnson, "Exxon Urges Developing Nations to Shun Environmental Curbs Hindering Growth," *Wall Street Journal*, October 14, 1997, p. B1.

52. Robert Engelman, *Stabilizing the Atmosphere* (Washington, D.C.: Population Action International, 1994), p. 34.

53. William K. Stevens, "Experts Doubt Rise of Greenhouse Gas

Will Be Curtailed," *New York Times*, November 3, 1997, p. A1.

54. Carl Haub, letter to author, January 15, 1997.

55. Rauber, "Heat Wave," pp. 38–39.

56. McKibben, *The End of Nature*.

57. "Climate Change: Greenpeace Pushes the End of Fossil Fuel," *Greenwire*, May 22, 1997.

58. Kerry Lund, letter to the editor, *E Magazine*, July–August 1997, p. 4.

59. Barbara Bonsignore, letter to the editor, *E Magazine*, November–December 1997.

60. McKibben, *The End of Nature*, p. 188.

61. Gregg Easterbrook, *A Moment on the Earth* (New York: Viking, 1995), p. 491.

PART THREE: NATION

Chapter Six

1. Barbara McMartin, *Hides, Hemlocks, and Adirondack History* (Utica, N.Y.: North Country Books, 1992), p. 148.

2. Ouida A. Girard, *Griffin: Ghost Town in the Adirondacks and Other Tales* (self-published, 1980), p. 24.

3. Donald Armstrong, interview, May 16, 1995.

4. Michael Pollan, *Second Nature: A Gardener's Education* (Boston: Atlantic Monthly Press, 1991), pp. 45–46.

5. Michael S. Teitelbaum and Jay M. Winter, *The Fear of Population Decline* (Orlando: Academic Press, 1985), p. 19.

6. Ibid., pp. 27–28.

7. Ibid., pp. 36–41.

8. Doug Bandow, "Dole's Military Card," *New York Times*, July 6, 1996, p. A21.

9. Myers, *Ultimate Security*, pp. 200–201.

10. Ben Wattenberg, "The Population Explosion Is Over," *New York Times Magazine*, November 23, 1997, p. 60.

11. Simon and Zinsmeister, "Population Growth," p. 73.

12. Lincoln H. Day and Alice Taylor Day, *Too Many Americans* (Boston: Houghton Mifflin, 1964), p. 134.

13. Barbara Crossette, "How to Fix a Crowded World: Add People," *New York Times*, November 2, 1997, sec. 4, p. 1.

14. Simon, pp. 269–70.

15. Thomas J. Espenshade and Jessie C. Gurcak, "Are More Immigrants the Answer to U.S. Population Aging?" *Population Today*, December 1996.

16. Peter G. Peterson, *Will America Grow Up Before It Grows Old?* (New York: Random House, 1996), p. 16.

17. Carl Haub, letter to author, January 15, 1997.

18. Peterson, p. 16.

19. Lester Thurow, *The Future of Capitalism: How Today's Economic Forces Shape Tomorrow's World* (New York: Morrow, 1996), p. 114.

20. Lester Thurow, "The Birth of a Revolutionary Class," *New York Times Magazine*, May 19, 1996, p. 46.

21. James Schulz, Allan Borowski, and William H. Crown, *The Economics of Population Aging: The Graying of Australia, Japan, and the United States* (Westport, Conn.: Auburn House, 1991), p. 338.

22. Roy Howard Beck, *Re-charting America's Future* (Petoskey, Mich.: The Social Contract Press, 1994), p. 90.

23. James Alan Fox, "The Calm Before the Juvenile Crime Storm?" *Population Today*, September 1996.

24. Richard Posner, *Aging and Old Age* (Chicago: University of Chicago Press, 1995).

25. Day and Day, p. 16.

26. Thurow, *The Future of Capitalism*, pp. 97–98.

27. World Bank, *Averting the Old Age Crisis: Policies to Protect the Old and Promote Growth* (New York: Oxford University Press, 1994), p. 160.

28. Jason Epstein, "White Mischief," *New York Review of Books*, October 17, 1996, p. 30.

29. Thurow, "The Birth of a Revolutionary Class."

30. Peterson, pp. 68–69.

31. Ibid., pp. 128–29.

32. World Bank, p. 50.

33. Arlie Russell Hochschild, *The Unexpected Community: Portrait of*

an *Old Age Subculture* (Berkeley: University of California Press, 1978), p. 28.

34. World Bank, p. 105.
35. Matthew Miller, "Three Social Security Myths," *New Republic*, April 15, 1996, p. 21.
36. Thurow, *The Future of Capitalism*, pp. 107–8.
37. Michael Tanner, "Public Opinion and Social Security Privatization," Cato Institute Web site, August 6, 1996.
38. Robert Dreyfuss, "The End of Social Security as We Know It," *Mother Jones*, November–December 1996, p. 50.
39. Peterson, p. 65.
40. Ibid., p. 77.
41. World Bank, p. 51.
42. Miller, p. 21.
43. Thurow, "The Birth of a Revolutionary Class."
44. Miller, p. 23.
45. World Bank, p. 2.
46. Peterson, pp. 48–49.
47. Schulz, Borowski, and Crown, pp. 228–29.
48. Lydia Bronte, *The Longevity Factor* (New York: HarperCollins, 1993), p. 21.
49. Thurow, *The Future of Capitalism*, p. 107.
50. Peterson, p. 137.
51. Bronte, p. 15.
52. Schulz, Borowski, and Crown, p. 124.
53. Hochschild, p. xii.
54. Bronte, pp. 334–35.
55. Schulz, Borowski, and Crown, p. 310.
56. Nicholas D. Kristof, "Aging World, New Wrinkles," *New York Times*, September 22, 1996, sec. 4, p. 1.
57. Lincoln Day, interview, June 11, 1996.
58. Betty Havers, "Canadian Long-Term Care Use," in Stanley R. Ingman et al., *An Aging Population, An Aging Planet, and a Sustainable Future* (Denton, Tex.: Center for Texas Studies, 1995), p. 91.
59. Tim Fried, "Millions More in Better Health as They Age," *USA Today*, March 18, 1997, p. A1.

60. Bronte, p. 10.
61. Kristof, "Aging World," sec. 4, p. 1.
62. Bronte, pp. 40–54.
63. Ibid., p. 90.
64. Teitelbaum and Winter, p. 108.
65. Day, interview.
66. Gail Sheehy, "New Passages," *Utne Reader,* May–June, 1996, p. 24.
67. Alan Wolfe, "The Age of Anxiety," *New Republic,* November 20, 1995, p. 26.
68. Hochschild, p. x.
69. "Urban Planning for the Ageing," *Canberra Times,* May 17, 1993.
70. Day, 1991, p. 25.
71. McKibben, *Hope,* p. 62.
72. Thurow, *The Future of Capitalism,* pp. 101–2.
73. Peterson, p. 114.
74. Ibid., p. 148.

Chapter Seven

1. Barbaralee Diamonstein, *The Landmarks of New York* (New York: Abrams, 1988), p. 173.
2. Beck, p. 122.
3. Federation for American Immigration Reform, pamphlet, 1996.
4. Robert Warren, "Immigration's Share of Population Growth," *Population Today,* September 1994.
5. "Immigration Restrictions Opposed by Sierra Club Leaders," Associated Press, October 17, 1997.
6. Robert McLure, "Enviro Groups Split over Open Door Policy," *Fort Lauderdale Sun-Sentinel,* August 29, 1997.
7. Jim Motovalli, "The Open-Door Policy: Are High Immigration Levels Hurting thé U.S. Economy—and the Environment?" *E Magazine,* September–October 1997, pp. 14–15.
8. David Durham, "USA: A Dissolving Culture?" *Carrying Capacity Network Focus* 6, no. 1 (1996): 8–9.
9. Richard Estrada, "Which Flag to Fly on the Fourth?" *Carrying Capacity Network Focus* 7, no. 1 (1997): 1.

10. Jason Din Alt, "A Not Particularly Modest Proposal That Would Solve America's Illegal Immigration Problem and Quite a Few Others," *Carrying Capacity Network Focus* 7, no. 1 (1997): 1.

11. Garrett Hardin, "Lifeboat Ethics," *BioScience* 24 (1974): 561.

12. Virginia Abernethy, "Changing the USA's Population Signals for a Sustainable Future," *Ecological Economics*, March 1994.

13. Edward Abbey, *One Life at a Time, Please* (New York: Holt, 1978).

14. Nicholas D. Kristof, "For Third World, Water Still a Luxury," *New York Times*, January 9, 1997, p. A1.

15. Celia W. Dugger, "Immigrant Influence Surges in New York City in the 90s," *New York Times*, January 9, 1997, p. A16.

16. Ralph Blumenthal, "Despite the Broadway Boom, Serious Plays Face Serious Peril," *New York Times*, January 9, 1997, p. C1.

17. Glenn Collins, "The Americanization of Salsa," *New York Times*, January 9, 1997, p. D1.

18. Spencer Abraham, William Bennett, Jack Kemp, and Malcolm Wallop, "A Manifesto for Immigration," *Wall Street Journal*, February 29, 1996, p. A18.

19. Todd S. Purdum, "A Resurgent California Finds All That Glitters Is Its Future," *New York Times*, September 3, 1997, p. A1.

20. Beck, pp. 142–43.

21. Ibid., p. 128.

22. Barbara Crossette, "How to Fix a Crowded World: Add People," *New York Times*, November 2, 1997, sec. 4, p. 1.

23. Dennis Hayes, *Population Press*, Spring 1995, p. 1.

24. Michael Maher, "Dodging Numbers—Reporters Avoid the Population Crunch," *Society of Environmental Journalists Journal* 7, no. 2 (Summer 1997), p. 1.

25. Lester Brown, *State of the World 1996* (Washington: Worldwatch Institute, 1996), p. 44.

26. Maher, "Dodging Numbers," p. 1.

27. Ibid., p. 3.

28. Benson Bobrick, *Angel in the Whirlwind* (New York: Simon & Schuster, 1997), p. 218.

29. Virginia Abernethy, *Population Politics: The Choices That Shape Our Future* (New York: Insight Books, 1993), p. 3.

30. Steven A. Holmes, "Public Cost of Teenage Pregnancy Is Put at $7 Billion This Year," *New York Times*, June 11, 1996.

31. Population Action International, *Reproductive Risk* (booklet) (Washington, D.C.: Population Action International, 1997), p. 1.

32. Alan Durning and Christopher Crowther, *Misplaced Blame: The Real Roots of Population Growth* (Seattle: Northwest Environment Watch, 1997).

33. Marilyn Hempel, "Misplaced Blame," *Population Press*, September–October 1997, p. 1.

34. Jennifer J. Cheek, *Mothers and Children at Risk: Adolescent Pregnancy Prevention in America*, White Paper No. 1 (Claremont, Calif.: Population Coalition, 1995), p. 3.

35. Daphne Spain and Suzanne M. Bianchi, "Most U.S. Unwed Mothers Are Not Teenagers," *Population Today*, November 1996.

36. Wattenberg, "The Population Explosion," p. 63.

37. Cheek, White Paper, p. 2.

38. John R. Weeks, "How to Influence Fertility: The Experience So Far," *NPG Forum*, 1990, p. 1.

39. R. G. Blumenthal, "Midlife Brooding: Some Parents Find Third Time a Charm," *Wall Street Journal*, March 29, 1996, p. 1.

40. Carl Haub, interview, November 6, 1997.

41. Beck, p. 57.

42. Ibid., p. 23.

43. Ibid., p. 14.

44. Gaylord Nelson, speech to Minnesota Wilderness Society, November 2, 1996.

45. "Sowing Preservation," *New York Times*, March 20, 1997, p. D1.

46. Victor Hull, "More People Are on the Way," *Sarasota Herald Tribune*, August 18, 1996, p. 1.

47. Wallace Stegner, "The Gift of Wilderness," in Stegner, *One Way to Spell Man: Essays with a Western Bias* (Garden City, N.Y.: Doubleday, 1982), p. 174.

48. Ibid., p. 170.

49. Boyd Wilcox, "Optimum Population and the Search for Stability," *Population Press* 2, no. 1, Fall 1995.

50. Paul Ehrlich and Anne Ehrlich, "The Most Overpopulated Nation," *NPG Forum*, 1991, p. 1.

51. David Pimentel and Marcia Pimentel, *Land, Energy, and Water: An NPG Forum* (Teaneck, N.J.: Negative Population Growth, 1989).

PART FOUR: SELF

Chapter Eight

1. Laura Duberstein Lindberg, "Young Men's Experience with Condom Breakage," *Family Planning Perspectives* 29, no. 3 (May–June 1997).

2. Suzanne Delbanco et al., "Public Knowledge and Perceptions About Unplanned Pregnancy and Contraception in Three Countries," *Family Planning Perspectives* 29, no. 2 (March–April 1997): 20.

3. Warren E. Leary, "Variety of Obstacles Is Blocking New Contraceptives," *New York Times*, May 29, 1996, p. A17.

4. Douglas Besharov, *Washington Post Weekly*, March 20–26, 1995.

5. Dorothy Stein, *Real World*, Spring 1993, p. 1.

6. David M. Feldman, *Marital Relations, Birth Control, and Abortion in Jewish Law* (New York: Schocken, 1974), p. 21.

7. Genesis 9:1, 7; 35:11.

8. Feldman, pp. 46–47.

9. Ibid., p. 50.

10. Robert Eisenberg, *Boychiks in the Hood: Travels in the Hasidic Underground* (New York: HarperCollins, 1995), p. 16.

11. Ehrlich, Ehrlich, and Daily, pp. 39–41.

12. 1 Corinthians 7:1–9.

13. John T. Noonan, *Contraception: A History of Its Treatment by the Catholic Theologians and Canonists* (Cambridge: Harvard University Press, 1996), p. 37.

14. Garrett Hardin, *Living Within Limits: Ecology, Economics, and Population Taboos* (New York: Oxford University Press, 1993), p. 105.

15. Noonan, pp. 110–11.

16. Ibid., p. 136.

17. Thomas Cahill, *How the Irish Saved Civilization* (New York: Anchor Books, 1996), pp. 66–67.

18. Noonan, pp. 164–65.

19. Ibid., pp. 187–88.
20. Feldman, p. 24.
21. Noonan, pp. 388–89.
22. Ibid., pp. 392–93.
23. Ibid., p. 409.
24. John Paul II, *Evangelium Vitae* (in English translation), *New York Times*, March 31, 1995, p. A16.
25. Carl Bernstein, "Holy Alliance: How Reagan and the Pope Conspired to Assist Poland's Solidarity Movement and Hasten the Demise of Communism," *Time*, February 24, 1992.
26. Joel E. Cohen, *How Many People Can the Earth Support?* (New York: Norton, 1995), p. 288.
27. Ehrlich, Ehrlich, and Daily, p. 125.
28. Jeanne Safer, *Beyond Motherhood: Choosing a Life Without Children* (New York: Pocket Books, 1996), pp. 8–9.
29. Ibid., pp. 20–25.
30. Ibid., p. 158.
31. Ibid., pp. 36–37.
32. Laurie Lisle, *Without Child: Changing the Stigma of Childlessness* (New York: Ballantine, 1996), p. 210.
33. Ibid., p. 37.
34. Gilbert Meilaender, "The Meaning of the Presence of Children," in Warren Cromartie, ed., *The Nine Lives of Population Control* (Grand Rapids: Eerdmans, 1995), p. 152.
35. John Berkman, "The Children of the Poor as Saving Remnant: John Ryan, Family Size, and the Common Good," paper delivered at the John Ryan Conference, September 14–17, 1995, University of St. Thomas, St. Paul, Minnesota.
36. Katha Pollitt, "Marooned on Gilligan's Island: Are Women Morally Superior to Men?" in Carol Bly, ed., *Changing the Bully Who Rules the World* (Minneapolis: Milkweed Editions, 1996), p. 138.
37. Alice Walker, "*One* Child of One's Own: A Meaningful Digression Within the Work(s)," in Janet Sternburg, ed., *The Writer on Her Work* (New York: Norton, 1980).
38. George Weigel, "What Really Happened at Cairo, and Why," in Warren Cromartie, ed., *The Nine Lives of Population Control* (Grand Rapids: Eerdmans, 1995), p. 140.

39. David L. Chandler, "Alaska Is Feeling the Heat," *Boston Globe*, September 14, 1997, p. C1.
40. Allan Gurganus, *Plays Well with Others* (New York: Pantheon, 1997), p. 316.
41. Sanford Dornbusch and Myra Strober, *Feminism, Children, and the New Families* (New York: Guilford Press, 1988), p. 37.
42. Kristin Luker, *Abortion and the Politics of Motherhood* (Berkeley, Calif.: University of California Press, 1984), pp. 169–70.
43. Ibid., pp. 186–87.
44. Scott Savage et al., "Family Is the Core: A Conversation," *Plain*, no. 11 (1996): 9.
45. Job 38:4, 8, 11, 25.
46. Luise Cardarelli, "The Lost Girls," *Utne Reader*, May–June 1996, pp. 13–14.
47. Kay Johnson, "The Politics of the Revival of Infant Abandonment in China, with Special Reference to Hunan," *Population and Development Review* 22, no. 1 (March 1996): 77–98.
48. Betsy Hartmann, *Reproductive Rights and Wrongs: The Global Politics of Population Control* (Boston: South End Press, 1995), p. 162.
49. Patrick Tyler, "Birth Control in China: Coercion and Evasion," *New York Times*, June 25, 1995, p. A1.
50. Hartmann, p. xv.
51. Steven W. Mosher, "Too Many People? Not by a Long Shot," *Wall Street Journal*, February 10, 1997, p. A18.
52. McKibben, *Hope*, p. 152.
53. Seth Faison, "Chinese Happily Breaking One-Child Rule," *New York Times*, August 17, 1997, p. A1.
54. McKibben, *Hope*, p. 155.
55. Hardin, *Living Within Limits*, p. 298.
56. Kenneth Boulding, "The Meaning of the Twentieth Century," in Hardin, *Living Within Limits*, p. 273.
57. Herman Daly and John Cobb, *For the Common Good: Redirecting the Economy Toward Community, the Environment, and a Sustainable Future* (Boston: Beacon Press, 1989), pp. 244–45.

Index